GOD, SOCIETY AND THE HUMAN PERSON

God, Society and the Human Person

The Basics of Catholic Social Teaching

EDWARD T. MECHMANN

ALBA·HOUSE   NEW·YORK

SOCIETY OF ST. PAUL, 2187 VICTORY BLVD., STATEN ISLAND, NEW YORK 10314

ST PAULS

Library of Congress Cataloging-in-Publication Data

Mechmann, Edward T.
    God, society and the human person: the basics of Catholic social teaching /
Edward T. Mechmann.
    p. cm.
    ISBN 0-8189-0886-6 (alk. paper)
    1. Sociology, Christian (Catholic) 2. Catholic Church. Catechismus Ecclesiae
Catholicae. 3. Catholic Church — Doctrines.   I. Title.

BX1753.M43 2000
261.8'088'22 — dc21

                                             00-040615

Produced and designed in the United States of America by the
Fathers and Brothers of the Society of St. Paul,
2187 Victory Boulevard, Staten Island, New York 10314-6603,
as part of their communications apostolate.

ISBN: 0-8189-0886-6

Printing Information:

Current Printing - first digit	1	2	3	4	5	6	7	8	9	10

Year of Current Printing - first year shown									
2000	2001	2002	2003	2004	2005	2006	2007	2008	2009

To Mary my Queen;
to Peggy my love; and
to Michael, Claire and Luke, my treasures.

Biblical Abbreviations

OLD TESTAMENT

Genesis	Gn	Nehemiah	Ne	Baruch	Ba
Exodus	Ex	Tobit	Tb	Ezekiel	Ezk
Leviticus	Lv	Judith	Jdt	Daniel	Dn
Numbers	Nb	Esther	Est	Hosea	Ho
Deuteronomy	Dt	1 Maccabees	1 M	Joel	Jl
Joshua	Jos	2 Maccabees	2 M	Amos	Am
Judges	Jg	Job	Jb	Obadiah	Ob
Ruth	Rt	Psalms	Ps	Jonah	Jon
1 Samuel	1 S	Proverbs	Pr	Micah	Mi
2 Samuel	2 S	Ecclesiastes	Ec	Nahum	Na
1 Kings	1 K	Song of Songs	Sg	Habakkuk	Hab
2 Kings	2 K	Wisdom	Ws	Zephaniah	Zp
1 Chronicles	1 Ch	Sirach	Si	Haggai	Hg
2 Chronicles	2 Ch	Isaiah	Is	Malachi	Ml
Ezra	Ezr	Jeremiah	Jr	Zechariah	Zc
		Lamentations	Lm		

NEW TESTAMENT

Matthew	Mt	Ephesians	Eph	Hebrews	Heb
Mark	Mk	Philippians	Ph	James	Jm
Luke	Lk	Colossians	Col	1 Peter	1 P
John	Jn	1 Thessalonians	1 Th	2 Peter	2 P
Acts	Ac	2 Thessalonians	2 Th	1 John	1 Jn
Romans	Rm	1 Timothy	1 Tm	2 John	2 Jn
1 Corinthians	1 Cor	2 Timothy	2 Tm	3 John	3 Jn
2 Corinthians	2 Cor	Titus	Tt	Jude	Jude
Galatians	Gal	Philemon	Phm	Revelation	Rv

Table of Contents

Preface

Catholic social teaching concerns the right ordering of society, so that its members may fulfill their earthly vocations and attain their eternal destiny. As such, it is a branch of moral theology, and is dedicated to the formation of conscience of those who are responsible for the organization of the human community.

The Church's involvement in social matters is a consequence of her nature and mission as the shepherd and steward of souls in their journey to salvation:

> The Church makes a judgment about economic and social matters when the fundamental rights of the person or the salvation of souls requires it. She is concerned with the temporal common good of men because they are ordered to the sovereign Good, their ultimate end. (*Catechism of the Catholic Church*, no. 2458. Hereafter, all references to the *Catechism* will appear in the text parenthetically by section number alone.)

This area of doctrine has a rich and venerable tradition, reaching back to the Apostolic age, and is highlighted by the writings of the greatest Catholic thinkers, such as St. Augustine and St. Thomas Aquinas. Social teaching has been the subject, either explicitly or implicitly, of Council documents and papal pronouncements throughout our history. In the last century the Church has been greatly endowed with powerful statements on society and its problems, from *Rerum Novarum* in 1891 through *Evangelium Vitae* in 1995.

Despite this history, however, Catholic social teaching has often been misunderstood or inadequately explained. The doctrines have occasionally been used to further partisan political agendas. They have been dismissed as being too theoretical for practical application to the "real" world, or for their reliance on supposedly outmoded philosophical and theological concepts. Others, for a variety of reasons, have tried to relegate these doctrines to the limited field of economic and social development, or have treated them as being so elastic that they could justify virtually any practical application. Few popular presentations of the teachings have placed them in their context within the full body of Catholic doctrine.

The *Catechism of the Catholic Church* provides a fine antidote to the state of confusion that currently exists regarding Catholic doctrine in general, and social teaching in particular. In many ways, the *Catechism* represents a pinnacle of Magisterial teaching on society, and the specific challenges faced by humanity in the present age. But in another sense, the *Catechism* is also an example of the importance of looking at fundamental principles as a way of understanding complex issues. By looking to this great compendium of doctrine, we can see the social teaching of the Church in its richest form — a body of dogma firmly rooted in the nature of the human person and his relationship with God, and in the salvific effect of God's grace in human life.

Unfortunately, if one were to look in the Index or Table

of Contents of the *Catechism* for the "Social Doctrine of the Church," one would be directed to a small section that deals primarily with economics, development, and love for the poor. While these are important components of the social doctrine, they certainly do not exhaust the field. The entries in the *Catechism*'s index under "Society," although broader in scope, are inadequate by themselves to encompass the full breadth of the Church's teachings on the ordering of the human community. To find the full body of Catholic social teaching, one must look to many sections of the *Catechism*.

The purpose of this book is to draw together these many disparate sections of the *Catechism*, and to organize Catholic social teaching into its major foundational principles and themes. The goal is to provide a reasonable overview of the social doctrines of the Church found in the *Catechism*, along with some examples of their practical application. It should also offer some indication of the relationship between the social doctrines and other dogmas of our faith.

Throughout this work, the words of the *Catechism* and other Church documents are extensively paraphrased or quoted, with a minimum of interpretation. This involves a sacrifice in the artfulness of the presentation, but I believe it is well justified, since the best way to understand the teaching of the Magisterium is to hear its own clear and unalloyed voice.

Before I begin, I would like to raise one preliminary point about terminology. The term "the human person" (or "the person," "humanity," "human beings" or "mankind") will be generally used to refer to human nature and human beings. However, with all due respect for those with concerns about "gender-inclusive" language, I have occasionally used terms such as "man," "he," "him," etc., particularly in quotations or close paraphrases from the *Catechism*, Church documents and Sacred

Scripture. These terms should be understood in their gender-neutral sense, to denote a human being, regardless of sex. They are used for two reasons. First, and most important, I believe it is inappropriate to tamper with the official translations of Church documents. But second, I did so primarily for stylistic purposes, to avoid tiresome repetition or awkward sentences.

I sincerely hope that this terminology will not present a barrier to anyone who seeks to use this little book to enhance their knowledge of Catholic social teaching. Obviously, the Church's understanding of human nature, and her moral doctrines, apply equally to males and females everywhere, regardless of the particular words used.

Having said that, let us begin our survey by looking at the fundamental basis for the Church's teachings on society — the nature of the human person.

CHAPTER ONE

Christian Anthropology:
The Nature of the Human Person

The starting point for the study of society must be with the human person. Throughout history, many schools of thought have proposed different views of the nature of humanity, stemming from varying sources. The classical theories of society — from Socrates, Plato and Aristotle through Hobbes, Locke, Rousseau and Marx — have all begun from a consideration of human nature. Catholic thought on society has followed this same approach. Indeed, as Pope John Paul II has noted, "the main thread and, in a certain sense, the guiding principle... of all of the Church's social doctrine, is a correct view of the human person and of his unique value" (*Centesimus Annus*, 11).

Unlike many other theories, however, the Catholic tradition is not a mere philosophical reflection. Rather, it focuses on the relationship between God and humanity. Because he is "created by God and for God" (27) and is endowed with "a spiritual and immortal soul" (1703), the human person cannot be properly comprehended without reference to his supernatural nature and destiny. Thus, the principles of Christian anthro-

1

pology are not derived from secular sciences alone — economics, sociology, and history cannot fully reveal the nature of humankind. Instead, the ultimate and complete truth about humanity must be sought in Divine Revelation — Sacred Scripture, the Tradition of the Church, and the teachings of the Magisterium (74 *et seq.*).

Of course, Revelation culminated and is definitively embodied in Jesus Christ, the Incarnate Word of God, the Second Person of the Trinity (73, 359). He is "the center of the universe and of history" (*Redemptor Hominis*, 1). As a result, Christian anthropology must ultimately be "Christo-centric" anthropology. This is of great significance to Catholic social doctrine, because Jesus is the model of true and perfect humanity, and the internal life of the Trinity is the model for the ideal life in community (520-21, 1878). Catholic social doctrine — just as all Catholic dogma — leads inevitably to Christ, and thereby to the Triune God.

An examination of the *Catechism* finds a number of general principles about human nature that can be found in Revelation and that form the underpinning of Catholic social teaching. This is not intended to be a comprehensive discussion of human nature as found in Revelation; rather, it is a brief outline of those characteristics that are most useful to understanding the social doctrines set forth in the *Catechism*.

1. THE HUMAN PERSON IS MADE IN THE IMAGE AND LIKENESS OF GOD.

From the creation account of Genesis we learn that "God created man in his image; in the divine image he created him" (Gn 1:27). Because the divine image is reflected in each individual, the human person holds special dignity in the order of creation (1702). This tenet of our faith is at the heart of the social teachings of the Church.

In addition, all human life is sacred because it is the product of the creative action of God from its very beginning, and remains in a special relationship with the Creator (2258). The human person is not a commodity, capable of being manipulated through historical, economic or social forces, or disposable at will. Rather, each individual participates in the nature and essence of God, and must be treated with the appropriate dignity and respect.

Human dignity comes primarily from being a child of God. This is in contrast with certain social theories (e.g., socialism or utilitarianism) that value people to the extent that they have instrumental usefulness, or that consider them to be mere components of society, the economy, or impersonal historical forces. It also is markedly opposed to the prevailing view of human life in Western secular culture, which would recognize as a person only those lives that are "wanted" while they are still in the womb, or those with a certain level of "quality of life" when they are frail. The Catholic perspective imposes a significant obligation on society to focus on the well-being and development of every human person.

2.   EACH HUMAN PERSON HAS A DESTINY OF
     LIFE EVERLASTING WITH GOD.

Because humanity was created with a spiritual and immortal soul, all are called to God Himself, and are destined for eternal life with Him (1878, 1703; cf., St. Augustine's famous prayer, "You made us for Yourself, and our hearts are restless until we rest in You."). The goal of human existence, the personal vocation of each individual, and the ultimate end of all human acts is to share in God's own holiness (1719). This destiny was called by a number of different names in Sacred Scripture (e.g., the "Kingdom of God"), but they all direct humanity to a sharing in the divine nature, the glory of Christ, and the joy of the life of the Trinity (1720, 1721).

Since the ultimate end of each human being is eternal life, political, social or economic achievement cannot be the entire focus of human activities or society's concerns (1723). Rather, spiritual and interior concerns must take precedence in the proper hierarchy of values (1886 *et seq.*). Society must be ordered with a primary emphasis on the spiritual and moral health of its members.

In living the life of holiness that strives to eternal life, the model is Christ Himself, "the perfect man" (521). All are unequivocally called to imitate Christ (459, 520). This duty, which must affect every aspect of life, has clear implications for organizing and participating in society.

This principle sharply separates Catholic thinking from Western intellectual trends. Few modern thinkers would recognize the ultimate supernatural destiny of humanity, or the reality of our relationship with the Creator. Rather, the prevailing view of humanity is that we are merely one animal among others, and if we are superior to them at all, it is only the product of an accident of evolutionary forces that have given us the power of reason. To this school of thought, the human person has no ultimate destiny. The meaning and significance of human life — or lack thereof — are limited to this world only.

3. HUMAN NATURE IS FLAWED BY ORIGINAL SIN AND IS INCLINED TO EVIL AND ERROR.

One cannot comprehend humanity or society without taking into account the profound and far-reaching reality of original and individual sin. "Sin is present in human history; any attempt to ignore it or to give this dark reality other names would be futile" (386). The Church resists modern tendencies to explain sin away, or to minimize its importance. "Without the knowledge Revelation gives of God we cannot recognize sin clearly and are tempted to explain it as merely a developmental flaw, a psychological weakness, a mistake, or the necessary consequence of an inadequate social structure, etc." (387). Overlooking the reality of original and individual sin would have significant deleterious consequences for human self-understanding. "Ignorance of the fact that man has a wounded nature inclined to evil gives rise to serious errors in the areas of education, politics, social action, and morals" (407).

Due to original sin, even though man desires to do good he is nevertheless "inclined to evil and subject to error" (1707). The consequences of original and individual sin are so prevalent that "the world is virtually inundated by sin" (401). It is sin that has produced the misery and oppression that humanity has experienced throughout history, in every social setting; there is a "universality of sin in human history" (401, 403, 1739). This sinful inclination remains in the heart of every person, even after the atonement of Christ and the cleansing grace of Baptism (405). Society is one of the fields in which humanity struggles with sin and evil, aided by God's grace (409).

The Church rejects the notion that evil exists in society as the result of impersonal forces or that it is not the responsibility of individuals. She cannot subscribe to Rousseau's idea that humanity by nature is in a state of original virtue, but society works to corrupt him. Nor can she accept the theory that human nature is thoroughly corrupt, either by nature or as the result of original sin, and can only be restrained by the power of society and government. Instead, the Church knows from Revelation that humanity is redeemed by the sacrifice of Christ, yet human nature remains flawed — "wounded in the natural powers proper to it; subject to ignorance, suffering, and the dominion of death; and inclined to sin…" (405).

4. ALL PERSONS ENJOY FREEDOM THAT MUST BE USED WITH MORAL RESPONSIBILITY.

Because we have been created in the divine image, human beings possess free will — "the power, rooted in reason and will, to… perform deliberate actions on one's own responsibility" (1731). This freedom is "an outstanding manifestation of the divine image," and is directed to drawing humanity closer to God (*Gaudium et Spes*, 17; cf. 1705, 1731).

It is crucial to note, however, that human freedom is limited and bears personal responsibility. It must be distinguished from prevailing notions of freedom in contemporary society that recognize neither restraints on human behavior nor any sense of accountability. Indeed, true freedom is always "in the service of what is good and just," while the choice to do evil is "an abuse of freedom and leads to the slavery of sin" (1733). Freedom is inextricably intertwined with the truth, and cannot be properly understood apart from it (1704, 1731, 1740; see also *Veritatis Splendor*, 31-34, and *Evangelium Vitae*, 18-19).

The use of freedom must also be understood to have personal moral consequences. The Catholic understanding of freedom entails that each person is called to make serious moral choices throughout his life and to choose good over evil (1706, 1723, 1732). "Freedom makes a man responsible for his acts to the extent that they are voluntary" (1734). Given man's intended destiny of eternal life, and the real possibility of eternal separation from God, his choices between good and evil are fraught with the most serious personal repercussions (1035, 1036).

Moreover, in the use of freedom, an individual cannot act as if he were alone and isolated. Freedom is exercised through relationships with others (1738, 1740). Freely chosen acts can be conducive to virtue in others, or they may contribute to the development of "structures of sin" in society that lead others to evil (1869). Freedom must therefore always be tempered by responsibility to others and to society as a whole.

5. THE HUMAN PERSON IS BY NATURE SOCIAL, AND IS UNITED TO THE ENTIRE HUMAN FAMILY.

It is an inherent characteristic of the human person to be in relation to others. Human beings are not only social in preference and desire, but it is necessary for us to live with others — "the human person needs to live in society" (1879). This is clear from the Genesis account of creation, where God declares, "it is not good for the man to be alone" (Gn 2:18). It is also implicit in the "new commandment" of Jesus that we love one another as He has loved us (1878, 1970). This aspect of human nature was recognized by the Fathers of the Second Vatican Council: "by his innermost nature man is a social being, and unless he relates himself to others he can neither live nor develop his potential" (*Gaudium et Spes*, 12). Through life in society, the human person develops in the fullest possible way, and responds most completely to his vocation (1879).

One human community was part of the divine plan from the time of creation — the family (2203). The family is "the natural society in which husband and wife are called to give themselves in love and in the gift of life" (2207). Because the family is prior to all other forms of society, it is the foundation for "freedom, security and fraternity within society" (2202, 2207). As a result, the family must be recognized, helped and defended by social authorities at every level (2202, 2209).

Moreover, because of our common origin in Adam, the human race forms a unity (360). This oneness is seen in humanity's shared nature, mission in life, earthly home, supernatural end, and redemption in Christ (360). No person can be excluded — in "this law of human solidarity and charity… all men are truly brethren" (361). This view of the relational nature of humanity has enormous significance to the Catholic understanding of society, particularly in its implications for the principles of subsidiarity and solidarity.

Much of modern philosophy and social theory, in contrast, relies on a conception of human nature that is fundamentally individualistic and utilitarian. This view regards people not as innately social, but rather as sociable by choice, depending on subjective evaluations of what is useful and satisfying. It tends to sever the necessary bonds that link persons into an organic society, and regards them as atomistic individuals, tied together only by their mutual agreement. This position is found in the social contract approach that underlies American constitutional thought, and the radical individualism that dominates modern Western intellectual circles.

6. BY WORK AND PRODUCTIVE ACTIVITY, EACH PERSON FULFILLS HIS NATURE AS A COOPERATOR IN CREATION.

The inclination to work and productive activity stems from the fact that the human person is created in the image of God, and is called to cooperate with and to extend the work of creation (2427). This is seen in Genesis, when God commanded Adam, "fill the earth and subdue it" (Gn 1:28). It is an extraordinary gift from God — the power to share in the divine plan by exercising dominion over the earth. God has enabled humanity "to complete the work of creation, to perfect its harmony for their own good and that of their neighbors" (307). Through their work, humans can thus truly be called "'God's fellow workers,' and co-workers for his kingdom" (307).

Work is not a punishment imposed due to Adam's primordial sin. It is a means of honoring the Creator and His gifts through the use of the talents given to us. It can also help us to attain our innate potential (2427, 2428). However, work is not the end of human nature. The value of labor stems from the nature of the human person, and is intended to serve people — "work is for man, not man for work" (2428).

CHAPTER TWO

The General Themes of Catholic Social Teaching

The *Catechism* sets forth many individual teachings on the human person and society, based on the core principles outlined above. These precepts can be organized into a number of themes.

A. SOCIETY IS AN ORGANIC ASSOCIATION DIRECTED TO THE BENEFIT OF THE PERSON.

Society is an association of people who are united by a principle that transcends each individual (1880). It is not merely an *ad hoc* conglomeration of individuals, but an organic reality, with a visible and spiritual life that extends through time, uniting the past to the present and reaching towards the future (1880). Each separate community is defined by its own purposes, and formulates its own rules of internal governance, but one rule is common to every society — "the human person... is and ought to be the principle, the subject, and the end of all social institutions" (*Gaudium et Spes*, 25; cf. 1881). Society is for humans, not vice versa (*Gaudium et Spes*, 26).

Both the family and the state are essential features of every society, because they correspond directly to human nature (1882). However, in order to promote the participation of all people in the affairs of society, the family and the individual cannot stand alone in relation to others and to the state. To that end, intermediate associations are needed in all areas, economic, social, religious, political, professional, and so forth. Examples of these organizations would include labor unions, trade associations, fraternal clubs, and political parties. These bodies advance the goal of "socialization," the natural human tendency to associate with others in order to obtain goals that are beyond the capacity of any one person. Socialization helps each person strengthen and develop their innate qualities, particularly their sense of initiative and responsibility, and also aids in protecting human rights (*Gaudium et Spes*, 25; cf. 1882).

Socialization enables individuals to attain their potential, but it also brings with it certain risks. As can be seen throughout history, but particularly clearly in the twentieth century, the state can easily assume powers that lead to excessive intervention in — and control over — individuals, threatening or destroying their freedom and initiative. In response to this threat, the Church has developed the principle of subsidiarity, according to which "a community of a higher order should not interfere in the internal life of a community of a lower order, depriving the latter of its functions, but rather should support it in case of need and help to co-ordinate its activity with the activities of the rest of society, always with a view to the common good" (*Centesimus Annus*, 48; 1883). Subsidiarity requires that matters should be left in the hands of families whenever possible, but when support is needed, the lowest level of government should take action (1894).

Subsidiarity sets limits on state power and its intervention in private affairs. It aims at regulating and harmonizing the relations between individuals and society, and establishing a just international order. It also "is opposed to all forms of collectivism" (1885). The most prominent concrete examples of collectivism in recent history are found in the economic policies of socialism and Communism. Likewise, certain aspects of the "social assistance state," more commonly known as the "welfare state," violate the principle of subsidiarity because they arrogate to the central authority activities that are properly the function of intermediate institutions or associations, and ultimately the family (see *Centesimus Annus*, 48-49).

The principle of subsidiarity is in many ways analogous to the American constitutional principle of federalism. Under a federalist arrangement, authority is divided between local and state governments and the federal government. So, the United States Constitution prescribes that certain powers are specifically or implicitly delegated to the national government, while others are reserved to the states or to the people. The composition of the legislative branch, and the way by which the President is elected, also reflect the effort to balance national and state power.

Although in theory American federalism reflects the principle of subsidiarity, it would be a mistake to equate the two in practice. There can be no question that the development of American constitutional law, especially since the 1930's, has resulted in a tremendous growth in the power exerted by the central government, to the detriment of state and local independence and initiative. This can be seen most clearly in the expansive interpretation given by the Supreme Court to the Commerce Clause, and in the "incorporation" of the Bill of Rights into the Fourteenth Amendment's Due Process Clause. Both of these developments have vastly expanded the federal government's — particularly the federal courts' — power to regulate matters that historically were left to local discretion, and to review and overturn actions of state and local governments. This has also been accompanied by a general decline in mediating institutions, such as fraternal organizations, trade unions, and so forth, and the emergence of a variety of threats to the integrity and health of families.

In addition, it should be noted that the principle of subsidiarity cannot be viewed in isolation, but must be considered in light of the common good and human solidarity. Thus, the principle of subsidiarity would not necessarily lend support to the complete devolution of power from central to local levels of government, without a searching analysis of whether such a transfer would serve the common good of all members of the community and advance the sense of solidarity in society. If such a rearrangement of authority were destructive of solidarity, or if it would unduly burden (or benefit) any segment of society, it would not be justifiable.

B. THE MORAL FOUNDATION FOR SOCIETY IS THE NATURAL LAW.

The natural law is one of the expressions of the moral law that governs Creation (1952). It is an expression of the Divine Will, inscribed on the human heart (1954). It is thus fundamental for humanity, society, and our relationship to God.

Natural law has been a subject for philosophical inquiry since the ancient Greeks, and has been at the center of the political and legal thought of Socrates, Aristotle, Cicero, Augustine, Aquinas, the masters of the English common law, and many, many others. See, e.g., Sophocles' *Antigone* ("These laws are not for now or for yesterday, they are forever"), Aristotle's *Nicomachean Ethics* ("What is natural has the same validity everywhere alike, independent of its seeming so or not"), and Cicero's *De Re Publica* ("True law... is universal; it is immutable and eternal... [A]ll nations will be subject all the time to this one changeless and everlasting law").

The natural law has fallen into some disfavor in certain Western intellectual circles since the Enlightenment, to the great impoverishment of our culture and laws. Yet without the natural law, society cannot be coherently understood.

"The natural law expresses the original moral sense which enables man to discern by reason the good and the evil, the truth and the lie" (1954). It "states the first and essential precepts which govern the moral life" (1955). Its principal tenets are expressed in the Ten Commandments, which has corollaries in many other cultures. "Present in the heart of each man and established by reason, [the natural law] is universal in its precepts and its authority extends to all men. It expresses the dignity of the person and determines the basis for his fundamental rights and duties" (1956). The application of the natural law may vary from culture to culture, depending on circumstances. Nevertheless, it is "immutable and permanent throughout the variations of history" (1958), and "remains a rule that binds men among themselves and imposes on them, beyond the inevitable differences, common principles" (1957). However, due to humanity's fallen nature, grace and revelation are needed to accurately and completely discern its precepts (1960).

The natural law is not just a collection of universal moral principles that govern individual conduct. It has important consequences for the ordering of society. It "provides the indispensable moral foundation for building the human community... [and] the necessary basis for the civil law" (1959). In order for

15

a civil law to be valid, it must not be in conflict with the natural law. Any law that does not comply with the natural law is no law at all, "and thus has not so much the nature of law as of a kind of violence" (St. Thomas Aquinas, *Summa Theologiae*, I-II, 93, 3, ad 2; quoted in 1902). A law that is contrary to the natural law is not binding, and should be resisted (1903, 2235, 2242). Relying in part on this principle, Pope John Paul II has declared that laws permitting abortion and euthanasia are invalid, and should be the object of conscientious resistance (*Evangelium Vitae*, 72-74). Similarly, laws that recognize slavery are equally invalid (see, e.g., *Gaudium et Spes*, 27).

The natural law thus serves both to construct the just society, and to protect all people from injustice.

C. SOCIETY IS ORDERED FOR THE COMMON GOOD.

Society is organized for the good of its members, both individually and collectively. "The dignity of the human person requires the pursuit of the common good. Everyone should be concerned to create and support institutions that improve the conditions of human life" (1926). Only if the common good is pursued can the dignity of humanity be achieved consistent with the principle of solidarity.

Given the social nature of humanity, the good of each individual is related to the common good, which itself can only be defined by reference to the individual human person (1905). The common good is defined as "the sum total of social conditions which allow people, either as groups or as individuals, to reach their fulfillment more fully and more easily" (*Gaudium et Spes*, 26; cf. 1906). It concerns the life of every individual in society, and requires prudence in moral and social decisions by every person and especially from those who hold authority (1906).

The common good contains three essential elements, each of which impose serious duties on public authority: respect for the person, social well-being and development, and peace. Respect for the person entails that the authorities in society must respect inalienable and fundamental human rights. In particular, the common good entails that society guarantee to each person the freedom to pursue their vocation in life. This would include ensuring freedom of religion, protecting the ability to act according to one's conscience, and safeguarding individual privacy (1907; see also *Gaudium et Spes*, 26).

Based on its concern for the dignity of the human person, who has been created in God's image, Catholic social teaching comes down decisively in support of natural human rights that cannot be justly denied by the state. These rights are innate and, by virtue of the unity of the human family, are possessed by all, regardless of national origin. This proclamation of the universality of human rights is a powerful rebuke to social and political structures that would deny people their just due. It also stands against those who regard social or political rights as dependent on the state's largesse alone, and subject to being arbitrarily withdrawn.

It is important to note, however, that these fundamental human rights are not just economic, social or political. Given our supernatural destiny and relationship with God, they must also include essential spiritual and moral rights — the ability to act according to conscience, and freedom of religion. No matter how open a political or economic system, the common good is incompatible with forcing people to act against their conscience or restricting their ability to worship God.

17

Second, the common good requires "the social well-being and development of the group itself" (1908). This entails the pursuit of prosperity in the spiritual and material goods of society (1925). Although the state must compromise between individual concerns that may be in conflict (e.g., through the political or judicial process), it must be done in the service of the common good and not to advance any ideology or narrow interest. Society may not favor particular social or economic groups in promoting development. Rather, all should have "ready access to all that is necessary for living: for example, food, clothing, housing, the right freely to choose his state of life and set up a family..." (*Gaudium et Spes*, 26; cf. 1908). The obligation to pursue development in the name of the common good is so significant that the *Catechism* denotes it as "the epitome of all social duties" (1908).

This notion of development and the common good is clearly distinct from the radical individualism that is at the heart of some strains of modern liberalism. This is especially true with regard to those that promote the market economy with few, if any, social or moral restraints. Certainly, economic libertarianism is incompatible with the social teaching of the Church. On the other hand, this principle plainly does not support a leveling kind of egalitarianism, which would impose an artificial economic parity on all, or a level of economic regulation that would render individuals or corporations as mere instruments of state planning and control. Instead, it recognizes the validity of the individual drive to economic and social development, but seeks to temper it by the dictates of human solidarity, which always calls each person to a serious concern for the happiness and fulfillment of all.

Development, of course, is not just economic or social — it must also address the spiritual nature of humanity. "An increased sense of God and increased self-awareness are fundamental to any full development of human society" (2441). Through this aspect of development, the increase in material goods is placed at the service of humanity and our freedom, which is, of course, linked directly with moral truth. Dire poverty and economic exploitation will be reduced, and people will be more open to the transcendent (2441). Therefore, true development advances the supernatural well-being of every human person.

The third essential element of the common good is peace, "that is, the stability and security of a just order" (1909). It is incumbent upon authority to guarantee the security of all members of society. In fact, the duty to maintain the common good is the rationale behind the legitimate right of collective and individual defense (1909). For instance, the right and obligation of the state to protect its citizens form the basis of the Church's qualified approval of capital punishment "if this is the only possible way of effectively defending human lives against the unjust aggressor" (2267). However, if "non-lethal means are sufficient to defend and protect people's safety... authority will limit itself to such means..." (2267). The *Catechism* goes on to state that as a result of the possibilities for preventing crime and incapacitating offenders, "the cases in which the execution of the offender is an absolute necessity 'are very rare, if not practically non-existent'" (2267, quoting *Evangelium Vitae*, 56).

It is important to note that the Church has emphasized that security must be maintained by morally acceptable means — peace cannot properly be guaranteed by unjust or immoral methods (1909). So, pursuing the security of society will not exonerate unjustly limiting or denying the fundamental rights of individuals, or the enactment of immoral legislation. For instance, governments that suspend civil liberties, ostensibly to address non-existent "national emergencies," are not pursuing the common good (2237).

In addition to these essential elements, there are several other aspects to the common good. Each community has its own common good that is particular to it. The realization of this unique common good is found in the political community. The state therefore has the obligation to defend and promote the common good of society, citizens, and intermediate associations (1910). The common good is also oriented to the progress of the human person, based on truth, justice and love (1912). Moreover, since society is organic, with a future and a past that transcends the individuals who comprise it, the common good must also have a regard for the well-being of future generations. Policies that would deprive one's descendants of material or social prosperity (e.g., a squandering of a people's cultural heritage or natural resources, or a ruinous national debt) would be inconsistent with the common good.

By virtue of the unity of the human race and the increasing interdependence of humanity, the common good also has a universal dimension that transcends borders. This implies the need for "an organization of the community of nations able to 'provide for the different needs of men,'" including such areas as food, hygiene, education, and the status of refugees and migrants (1911, quoting *Gaudium et Spes*, 84). Indeed, the Church has long been one of the firmest supporters of the ideals of cooperation in the international community, and for the United Nations in particular (despite its evident flaws).

Note that the common good is not the mere sum of the individual goods of each member of society, as would be proposed by the utilitarians. Rather, it aims to satisfy the dignity of each individual, and of society as a whole. The common good would thus not be served by ordering society to the advantage of any one group or class, or by imposing a false egalitarianism on disparate people. Rather, social decisions must be made with regard to the genuine development of all.

D. SOCIETY MUST PROMOTE THE SPIRITUAL GOOD OF THE HUMAN PERSON.

It is crucial to Catholic teaching to take into account that society is both visible and spiritual (1880). As a result, the proper hierarchy of values must be respected, which "subordinates physical and instinctual dimensions to interior and spiritual ones" (1886). In ordering society, then, we must understand not just economic, political and social policy, but the impact of sin and the need for inner conversion.

Due to the reality and consequences of original and individual sin, society cannot be idealized as a perfect community. All societies are imperfect, just as fallen humanity is imperfect. This imperfection is the result, and the further cause, of sin (379, 408, 1740). "Sins give rise to social situations and institutions that are contrary to the divine goodness. 'Structures of sin' are the expression and effect of personal sins. They lead their victims to do evil in their turn. In an analogous sense, they constitute a 'social sin'" (1869; quoting *Reconciliatio et Paenitentia*, 16). This point is powerfully illustrated by Pope John Paul II's analysis of "the culture of death" in *Evangelium Vitae*.

As a result of these "social sins," society must be involved in an "appeal to the spiritual and moral capacities of the human person and to the permanent need for his inner conversion, so as to obtain social changes that will really serve him" (1888). This inner conversion is not merely a call to a greater

21

private exercise of piety. Rather, it has profound consequences for the role of the Christian in society. It "imposes the obligation of bringing the appropriate remedies to institutions and living conditions when they are an inducement to sin, so that they conform to the norms of justice and advance the good rather than hinder it" (1888). Hence, there is an affirmative duty on the Christian to shape society in a way that advances justice and eliminates the causes and occasions of sin.

The heart of any social reform is charity, "that is, love of God and of neighbor," because "charity is the greatest social commandment" (1889). For the Christian who is addressing the problems of society, then, the answers are not to be found exclusively in the secular sciences. "There can be no genuine solution of the social question apart from the Gospel" (*Centesimus Annus*, 5; cf. 1896).

It is impossible to overstate the importance of this spiritual dimension of Catholic social teaching. The Church is not a private social services agency, a political action committee, or an institution dedicated to education in the secular arts and sciences. She legitimately performs many of those functions, but "all the activities of the Church are directed, as toward their end, to the sanctification of men in Christ and the glorification of God" (*Sacrosanctum Concilium*, 10; quoted in 824). As Pope John Paul II has said, "a man's true identity is only fully revealed to him through faith, and it is precisely from faith that the Church's social teaching begins. While drawing upon all the contributions made by the sciences and philosophy, her social teaching is aimed at helping everyone on the path of salvation" (*Centesimus Annus*, 54).

Those who interpret and implement Catholic social teaching must be on their guard to avoid giving the faithful the impression that it is directed merely to the amelioration of the human condition, the redistribution of wealth, or the accomplishment of partisan political goals. Likewise, we must be careful not to fall into the belief that the pursuit of social justice is itself sufficient to attain salvation. That would run the risk of allowing Pelagianism to insinuate itself into our thought. (The heresy of Pelagianism, which flourished in the fifth century but persists in many forms to this day, held that people can achieve salvation through their own unaided powers.) Catholic doctrine is dedicated to the salvation of souls. This salvation comes by the grace of God through the Passion of Our Lord Jesus Christ, not through human efforts to improve society (1987 ff.).

At the same time, it would be a mistake to consider the Church's teaching on society to have only a spiritual dimension. This would imply that the material well-being of men is of little consequence, so long as their spiritual needs are satisfied. If taken to its extreme, the excessive spiritualization of Catholic social teaching would consign people to temporal misery, while offering them only the consolation of bliss in the next life and the assurances that they will be prayed for. This runs directly contrary to the specific injunctions of Revelation that we must care for those in need (see, e.g., Mt 25:31-46 and Jm 1:15-17), and to the example of Jesus Himself, who was "moved with pity" by human suffering (see, e.g., Mt 15:32). Pope John Paul II has spoken authoritatively on this very point: "As far as the Church is concerned, the social message of the Gospel must not be considered a theory, but above all else a basis and a motivation for action" (*Centesimus Annus*, 57).

Clearly, the proper attitude is one that balances the temporal and spiritual aspects of the social doctrines, while still recognizing that the latter hold precedence.

E. A FUNDAMENTAL END OF SOCIETY IS SOCIAL JUSTICE.

Closely linked to the common good is the goal of social justice. "Society ensures social justice when it provides the conditions that allow associations or individuals to obtain what is their due, according to their nature and vocation" (1928). The basis for social justice is respect for the transcendent dignity of the human person, created in the image of God (1929). This means that public authority must respect natural human rights (1930). It also requires fostering in society a fraternal sense — "everyone should look upon his neighbor (without any exception) as 'another self,' bearing in mind above all his life and the means necessary for living it in a dignified way" (*Gaudium et Spes*, 27; cf. 1931). This duty is particularly compelling with regard to the disadvantaged, and to those who "think or act differently from us" (1932, 1933). This stems directly from Jesus' specific and challenging injunctions in the Gospel, even to the point of forgiving offenses and foregoing the natural human tendency to hate one's enemies (1933; see, e.g., Mt 5:43-44).

Social justice also requires dealing with the equalities and differences among people. All people are equal in their dignity and nature, and thus in the rights that flow from them (1934, 1935). "Forms of social or cultural discrimination in basic personal rights on the grounds of sex, race, color, social conditions, language, or religion must be curbed and eradicated as incompatible with God's design" (*Gaudium et Spes*, 29; cf. 1935). However, it is undeniable that individual men and women are born with differences in physical, material, intellectual and moral abilities (1936). Although these differences are part of God's plan, it is incumbent that these "talents" be shared with those who are in need of them. "These differences encourage and often oblige persons to practice generosity, kindness, and sharing of goods" (1937). It is also necessary that sinful inequalities, which are "in open contradiction of the Gospel," be eliminated, such as "excessive economic and social disparity between individuals and peoples of the one human race" (*Gaudium et Spes*, 29; cf. 1938, 1947). There is, therefore, a serious obligation of personal action to foster justice in society through the proper husbanding and sharing of one's abilities and resources.

The search for social justice entails the fundamental notion of human solidarity. This principle "also articulated in terms of 'friendship' or 'social charity,' is a direct demand of human and Christian brotherhood" (1939). Solidarity stems from the shared origin of each person at the creative hand of God, his equality of nature, and the common redemption in the sacrifice of Jesus Christ (1939). It is expressed in many areas, but always works against the radical individualism that has infiltrated modern life. It first appears in the distribution of goods and remuneration for work, but also involves the effort to build a more just social order, "where tensions are better able to be reduced and conflicts more readily settled by negotiation" (1940). Social problems cannot be resolved without solidarity across the many divisions between men — uniting the poor among themselves, rich and poor, workers and their employers, and different peoples (1940). Ultimately, this "eminently Christian virtue" reaches beyond borders — "international solidarity is a requirement of the social order; world peace depends in part upon this" (1941, 1948). As with every aspect of Catholic social teaching, solidarity is focused not merely on material goods, but on the sharing of spiritual goods as well (1948).

Social justice can be a difficult concept. For many Americans, steeped in the traditions of the common law, legal positivism and economic liberalism, "justice" tends to be conceived in procedural, rather than substantive terms. In this sense, "justice" means that one has been afforded a fair process, not necessarily that the result is "just" when evaluated against an objective standard. So, Americans tend to stress ideas such as "equal protection under the law," "due process of the law," open proceedings with adequate representation, and so on. In the economy, justice would be associated with equal opportunity, non-discrimination, open competition, and a meritocracy. A just economic system would be one in which all have an equal chance to compete, without taking into account the result of that competition.

The Church does not recognize such a distinction between substance and procedure. Social justice is not merely a hortatory ideal. For this doctrine to have any meaning, there must be a serious effort to ensure that living conditions are improved for all, and a sense of true solidarity must permeate social and individual relations. Wherever economic and social disparities exist, especially when they are extreme or glaring, they must be examined carefully to see if they violate social justice. Efforts must be made constantly to promote justice in all of our social and economic relationships. "The Church's stand on social justice is firm: Charity is required. And once the principle is recognized, it has manifold implications in every aspect of human living."[1]

It is also important to note that social justice cannot be achieved solely through legislative or regulatory action by the state. Justice is fundamentally a relational virtue, and presupposes freedom on the part of the actor. It cannot be coerced or imposed from above without sacrificing some degree of politi-

---

[1] John A. Hardon, S.J., *The Catholic Catechism* (Garden City: Doubleday, 1975), 389.

cal and economic freedom. "Justice toward men disposes one to respect the rights of each and to establish in human relationships the harmony that promotes equity with regard to persons and to the common good" (1807). Social justice is embodied in and is a result of a multitude of individual decisions and actions (e.g., business and financial dealings, electoral votes, etc.). State action, of course, has a crucial role to play, since the law can promote, encourage and reward justice and equity in private relations, and thereby create a climate conducive to virtue. However, "regulating [the economy] solely by the law of the marketplace fails social justice, for 'there are many human needs which cannot be satisfied by the market'" (2425, quoting *Centesimus Annus*, 34). Ultimately, social justice cannot be attained without a conversion of heart by individuals, which will then impel them to seek positive social change through the reform of institutions and conditions (1888).

Indeed, some secular theorists have argued forcefully that the pursuit of "social justice" through mandated income redistribution and government intervention is inherently incompatible with economic and political freedom (see, e.g., the writings of Nobel laureate economist Friedrich von Hayek). Certainly, the Church's consistent condemnation of collectivism (see, e.g., 1885, and *Centesimus Annus*, 41) must be considered whenever social justice is pursued through the dictates of the state.

However one applies these principles to concrete social situations, one thing is quite clear from the teachings of the Church: the common good cannot be attained without social justice.

F.   HUMAN LIFE MUST BE PROTECTED BY SOCIETY.

The fundamental, integral human right is the right to life. From the moment of conception, every human being is entitled to recognition of his rights as a person, and must be protected absolutely (2270). This tenet of Catholic dogma stems directly from the fact that each human person has been created in the image and likeness of God Himself, which bestows upon him "the dignity of a person, who is not just something, but someone" (371). It inheres in man's spiritual nature and destiny — "from his conception, he is destined for eternal beatitude" (1703). All the foundational principles of the Church's social teaching — social justice, solidarity, the common good, the natural law — cry out that the right to life cannot be trodden upon.

"The inalienable right to life of every innocent human individual is a constitutive element of a civil society and its legislation" (2273). Human life must be respected and protected by society and by political authorities. These human rights "belong to human nature and are inherent in the person by virtue of the creative act from which the person took his origin" (Sacred Congregation for the Doctrine of the Faith, *Donum Vitae*, III; cf. 2273). They are not bestowed upon a person by laws, constitutions, or courts. Nor are they revocable at the will of the state — that would be a grave injustice. "The moment a positive law deprives a category of human beings of the protection which civil legislation ought to accord them, the state is denying the equality of all before the law... [and] the very foundations of a state based on law are undermined" (*Donum Vitae*, III; cf. 2273). In recognition of the danger of threats against the unborn, the Church states clearly that "as a consequence of the respect and protection which must be ensured for the unborn child from the moment of conception, the law must provide appropriate penal sanctions for every deliberate violation of the child's rights" (*Donum Vitae*, III; cf. 2273).

The application of these principles to concrete issues in society is clear. Abortion — the "unspeakable crime" (*Gaudium et Spes*, 27) — cannot be tolerated by any society that aspires to justice (2322). Other violations of the right to life, such as murder (2268 ff.), euthanasia (2276 ff.), assisted suicide (2280 ff.), and fetal experimentation (2274-75), are equally abhorrent to human nature and the moral law (see also *Evangelium Vitae, passim*). Any laws that permit such practices (such as those of the United States that permit abortion on demand at any time of pregnancy) are gravely contrary to the divine and natural laws, and are thus invalid. Such a law "has not so much the nature of law as of a kind of violence" (1902, quoting St. Thomas Aquinas). No one is required in conscience to obey such unjust laws (1903, 2235, 2242). In specific terms, with respect to laws that allow abortion on demand, assisted suicide, euthanasia, fetal experimentation and so forth, no one can accept their legitimacy or cooperate in their execution (see *Evangelium Vitae*, 74).

In his magnificent encyclical, *Evangelium Vitae*, Pope John Paul II probes deeply into the grave threats to human life in modern society. He identifies a "veritable structure of sin" that stems from a "climate of widespread moral uncertainty":

> This reality is characterized by the emergence of a culture which denies solidarity and in many cases takes the form of a veritable "culture of death." This culture is actively fostered by powerful cultural, economic and political currents which encourage an idea of society excessively concerned with efficiency....

[I]t is possible to speak in a certain sense of a war of the powerful against the weak: a life which would require greater acceptance, love and care is considered useless, or held to be an intolerable burden, and is therefore rejected in one way or another. A person who, because of illness, handicap or, more simply, just by existing, compromises the well-being or life-style of those who are more favored tends to be looked upon as an enemy to be resisted or eliminated. In this way a kind of "conspiracy against life" is unleashed. (*Evangelium Vitae*, 12)

The pervasiveness of the "culture of death" in modern society, particularly in the democracies of the West, cannot be understated — nor can its insidious danger. Lurking behind superficially attractive slogans that appeal to one's sense of freedom and autonomy, or that make claims against one's natural sympathy for "hard cases," the culture of death undermines the foundations of civil society. It strikes at the heart of social justice and solidarity.

Nor can we stand idly by while innocent human lives are destroyed under the guise of the law, or hide behind "pluralism" and the incoherent notion that one cannot "impose morality" on others. Our duty is clear:

This situation, with its lights and shadows, ought to make us all fully aware that we are facing an enormous and dramatic clash between good and evil, death and life, the "culture of death" and the "culture of life." We find ourselves not only "faced with" but necessarily "in the midst of" this conflict: we are all involved and we all share in it, with the inescapable responsibility of choosing to be unconditionally pro-life. (*Evangelium Vitae*, 28)

G. ALL MEMBERS OF SOCIETY HAVE RIGHTS AND RESPONSIBILITIES.

Each individual member of society has fundamental rights and duties that conform to and stem from their human dignity. The first of these is to full and responsible participation in society.

"'Participation' is the voluntary and generous engagement of a person in social interchange. It is necessary that all participate, each according to his position and role, in promoting the common good. This obligation is inherent in the dignity of the human person" (1913). The right and duty of participation stems from humanity's communal nature. Since each human is inherently a being who is in relation to others, we can only satisfy our nature by associating with others and joining in with mutual activities. The primary field for exercising this right is in those areas over which one has personal responsibility. "By the care taken for the education of his family, by conscientious work, and so forth, man participates in the good of others and of society" (1914). People must also become involved in public affairs, within the particular circumstances of their country and culture (1915). Public authority must encourage participation and service by all, beginning with education and culture (1917).

Genuine participation is impossible without information. To an increasing extent, people are dependent on the communications media for this information, and they must be prudent in using it to form enlightened and correct consciences (2496).

As a result, "the information provided by the media is at the service of the common good. Society has a right to information based on truth, freedom, justice, and solidarity" (2494). The Church clearly prefers open communication as a way to ensure full participation in society by all citizens. It is doubtful that the media in any country presently satisfies these standards.

In addition to responsible participation, people have certain specific rights and obligations within the community. They are obligated to respect those in authority "as representatives of God," and to obey the established laws (2238, 2240). However, all persons have the right, and occasionally the duty, "to voice their just criticisms of that which seems harmful to the dignity of persons and to the good of the community" (2238). Citizens must also contribute to the good of society, based on a sense of love and service to one's country (2239). "Submission to authority and co-responsibility for the common good make it morally obligatory to pay taxes, to exercise the right to vote, and to defend one's country" (2240). Those who live in the relatively more prosperous nations are also required to welcome foreigners who seek security and a way of earning their livelihood. Political authorities may, however, impose reasonable conditions on the welcoming of immigrants (2241). All persons, especially journalists, must use the means of social communication for the common good, which requires a commitment to truth and respect for the moral law and the dignity of mankind (2494 *et seq.*).

The duty of respectful submission to authority is not without limits. It can never justify a blind obedience to the dictates of government, without regard to content — a Christian cannot responsibly seek justification in the claim that he was "just following orders." As discussed above, unjust laws are not valid, or binding in conscience (see, e.g., 2242). Thus, "the citizen is obliged in conscience not to follow the directives of civil authorities when they are contrary to the demands of the moral order, to the fundamental rights of persons or the teachings of the Gospel" (2242). Civil disobedience has a firm foundation in Catholic social teaching.

The duty of civil disobedience, however, does not justify armed resistance against the state, unless certain strict conditions are all satisfied:

"(1) there is certain, grave, and prolonged violation of fundamental rights;
(2) all other means of redress have been exhausted;
(3) such resistance will not provoke worse disorders;
(4) there is well-founded hope of success; and
(5) it is impossible reasonably to foresee any better solution" (2243).

It stands to reason that one must exercise a high level of prudence, and rigorously examine the moral legitimacy of one's decision, before pursuing a course of armed rebellion against civil authorities. Some instances of armed rebellion are clearly justified under these conditions, such as the American Revolution, or the French Resistance against the collaborationist Vichy regime and the Nazi forces of occupation during World War II. Others are plainly illegitimate, such as the secession of the southern American states in 1861 (which certainly failed to satisfy the first two conditions, in addition to which the secession was dedicated to preserving the gross injustice of slavery) or the campaigns of urban terrorism by radicals in the United States during the 1970's and 1980's and the terrorist bombing of the federal office building in Oklahoma City in 1995 (which plainly violated each condition). Other rebellions are more difficult to assess. For example, the 1956 revolution in Hungary was justified by the manifest and persistent injustices of the Communist regime. But it may have been doomed to failure and thus to produce brutal reprisals by the Soviet occupation forces, even without the inaction of the Western powers, whom the rebels had hoped would intervene. Heroism in a just cause does not always guarantee moral rectitude.

Underlying these important civic responsibilities is the paramount obligation of every person continually to seek inner conversion, "so as to obtain social changes that will really serve him" (1888). Thus, in all social activities, there is a serious duty to live a life of virtue and charity. There can be no hiding behind — or blaming — "systems," "rules" or "policies." Everyone is responsible for the extent to which he contributes to, or detracts from, the justice and morality of society, for "there are no just structures without people who want to be just" (2832).

H. PUBLIC AUTHORITY HAS IMPORTANT DUTIES AND POWERS TO PROMOTE THE COMMON GOOD.

Public authority is essential to the proper functioning of society. It derives from the social nature of humanity (1898). "Human society can be neither well-ordered nor prosperous unless it has some people invested with legitimate authority to preserve its institutions and to devote themselves as far as is necessary to work and care for the good of all" (*Pacem in Terris*, 46; 1897). Authority means "the quality by virtue of which persons or institutions make laws and give orders to men and expect obedience from them" (1897). Ultimately, all authority derives from God (1899).

The role of authority in society is to ensure the common

good (1898). It must dedicate itself to pursuing the common good of society by morally legitimate means (1902, 1903). It must be "a moral force based on freedom and a sense of responsibility" (1902). Preferably, the structure of public authority would reflect a balance between powers and "spheres of responsibility which keep it within proper bounds. This is the principle of the 'rule of law,' in which the law is sovereign and not the arbitrary will of men" (*Centesimus Annus*, 44). The organization of state authority must also conform to the principle of subsidiarity (1883, 1894). The teaching of the Church would thus tend to favor constitutional structures like the Anglo-American separation of powers between branches and levels of government, with an independent judiciary to ensure the accountability of the state.

It must be noted, however, that Catholic social teaching does not mandate any particular form of government. Rather, "the choice of the political regime and the appointment of rulers are left to the free decision of the citizens" (*Gaudium et Spes*, 74). Different forms of government may be morally acceptable, so long as they "serve the legitimate good of the communities that adopt them" (1901). However, if a regime were by nature "contrary to the natural law, to the public order, and to the fundamental rights of persons" it could not serve the common good and would thus be illegitimate (1901). These principles would implicitly require political structures that rest their legitimacy on the consent of the governed — popular sovereignty of some kind. They would exclude regimes that came to power as the result of usurpations or conquest, like the Fascist regimes in Germany, Italy and Spain, the Communist regimes of Eastern Europe before 1990, or the series of military juntas that have ruled many countries in the developing world, such as Nigeria, Argentina or Bolivia.

There are also strict limits on the behavior of governments. As we have already noted, the state must avoid despotic behavior, respect the fundamental rights of persons, and not "enact unjust laws or take measures contrary to the moral order"; such violations of the natural law render the state's acts invalid (1902, 1903, 2235, 2237). One concrete example of this limitation is that the state may not suspend political rights without legitimate and proportionate reasons (2237). So, for instance, the series of laws enacted in the 1930's by the Nazi regime that suspended the civil and political rights of Jews were contrary to the natural moral law principle against unjust discrimination, and were thus fundamentally invalid. Likewise, the "Jim Crow" laws enforced in America after Reconstruction and until the 1960's, which restricted the right to vote and effected a separation of the races, were similarly void.

This idea of limited government is crucial to Catholic social thought. It stands in bold contrast to the positivist view of the law, prevalent in Western society since the Enlightenment and dominant in contemporary American legal circles. The positivist approach would ultimately recognize no boundaries to the decisions made through the political process, except those that transgress previously-agreed limits (e.g., the provisions of a constitution). The candid positivist, for instance, would even recognize the legitimacy and binding force of the laws of the Nazi regime, even while deploring their content.

This point is not merely academic and historical, but has a very real application in concrete, contemporary legal disputes. For example, Justice Antonin Scalia of the United States Supreme Court, in remarks made at the Gregorian University in Rome (reported in *Origins* 26.6 [6/27/96]), affirmed the validity of unjust laws that are enacted through a democratic process, and the duty of jurists to uphold them, regardless of their individual beliefs. In this positivist legal environment, the will of the people, expressed through the democratic process, is sovereign and not accountable to any higher law. In effect, as Pope John Paul II has noted, this notion of radical majority rule can lead to the creation of a "tyrant state, which arrogates to itself the right to dispose of the life of the weakest and most defenseless members, from the unborn child to the elderly, in the name of a public interest which is really nothing but the interest of one part. The appearance of the strictest respect for legality is maintained.... Really what we have here is only the tragic caricature of legality; the democratic ideal, which is only truly such when it acknowledges and safeguards the dignity of every human person, is betrayed in its very foundations..." (*Evangelium Vitae*, 20, emphasis in original omitted).

In contrast, the Catholic view is that government is constrained by natural law and dedicated to the common good. This is the prescription for truly limited government. Indeed, unless society recognizes a higher law, there is ultimately no limit to the power of the state. Without the natural law, as Aquinas stated, "whatever the prince wills, is the law" (*Summa Theologiae*, I-II, 90, 1, ad 3).

Catholic social teaching recognizes that there are a number of important functions that must be performed by public authority in the pursuit of the common good. In general terms, the exercise of authority is a service, and "is meant to give outward expression to a just hierarchy of values in order to facilitate the exercise of freedom and responsibility by all" (2236). It is also important to recall that governments are not ends in themselves, but rather are instruments by which people can order their lives together and work towards their ultimate end — life eternal with God.

With these principles in mind, the duties and powers of

the government are seen in the *Catechism* to include:

- Defending human life (see paragraph F, above).
- Helping and defending the family (see paragraph L, below).
- Guaranteeing the right of religious liberty (see paragraph M, below).
- Regulating the exercise of the right to own private property, for the sake of the common good (see paragraph I, below).
- Ensuring the security necessary for citizens to conduct economic activity (2431, see paragraph J, below).
- Practicing distributive justice in a manner that takes into account "the needs and contributions of each, with a view to harmony and peace" (2236).
- Preserving peace and security within society and in the international community, and defending the nation and its citizens against threats from within and without (2263-67 and 2302-17; see paragraph K, below).
- Promoting living conditions "that allow [citizens] to grow and reach maturity: food and clothing, housing, health care, basic education, employment, and social assistance" (2288).
- Orienting the demographics of the population, but only through means that do not violate the moral law. "This can be done by means of objective and respectful information, but certainly not by authoritarian, coercive measures. The state may not legitimately usurp the initiative of spouses, who have the primary responsibility for the procreation and education of their children" (2372). The odious population control policies pursued by the Chinese

government (e.g., forced abortion and sterilization) provide a clear example of the dangers inherent in this area.

- Preventing the establishment of "laws or social structures leading to the decline of morals and the corruption of religious conduct," or that make a virtuous life difficult (2286). One example would be by preventing the production and distribution of indecent and obscene materials (2354) or restricting legalized gambling (cf. 2413). Until recent years, this was universally recognized in the United States as a proper and imperative function of the state, but is now largely ignored.

- Defending and protecting a "true and just freedom of information" in the various means of social communications. This would include protecting public morality and the rights of individuals to reputation and privacy (2498). It is particularly important for the state to refrain from the use of "disinformation for manipulating public opinion through the media" (2498). The *Catechism* expressly censures the conduct of totalitarian regimes that "systematically falsify the truth, exercise political control of opinion through the media, manipulate defendants and witnesses at public trials, and imagine that they secure their tyranny by strangling and repressing everything they consider 'thought crimes'" (2499). One can easily recognize the history of the twentieth century, particularly Communist and Fascist regimes, in this condemnation.

In fulfilling these duties and exercising these powers, specific legislative acts will, of course, depend on the circumstances that prevail in each separate community. However, if public authority adheres to the natural law, it will be able genuinely to advance the common good.

I. THE MATERIAL GOODS OF THE WORLD ARE
    ENTRUSTED TO HUMANITY FOR THE BENEFIT
    OF ALL, ESPECIALLY THE POOR.

It is the legacy of God's creation of the world that the earth
and its resources are entrusted "to the common stewardship of
mankind to take care of them, master them by labor, and enjoy their fruits" (2402). These goods of creation "are destined
for the whole human race" (2402). The Church calls this "the
universal destination of goods."

This is not to say, however, that all the resources of the
world must be held in common. Instead, "the promotion of the
common good requires respect for the right to private property and its exercise" (2403). This right is "legitimate for guaranteeing the freedom and dignity of persons and for helping
each of them to meet his basic needs and the needs of those in
his charge" (2402). From this right, a sense of solidarity should
develop, leading people to understand their relationship with
others (2402). Hence, the right to own and use property should
be exercised as a matter of stewardship, with an understanding that property should benefit not just its owner, but others
as well. "The ownership of any property makes its holder a steward of Providence, with the task of making it fruitful and com-
municating its benefits to others, first of all his family" (2404).
To ensure that property is used in a manner consistent with the
common good, public authority has the right and duty to regulate it (2406).

These principles have special implications for the way in
which society deals with the poor and promotes social justice.
It is a specific, clear and normative teaching of Sacred Scripture and the Tradition of the Church that humanity has a special duty to care for the poor. This mandate "is inspired by the

Gospel of the Beatitudes, of the poverty of Jesus, and of his concern for the poor" (2444). It is emphasized and strengthened by the sacramental life of the Church. "The Eucharist commits us to the poor. To receive in truth the Body and Blood of Christ given up for us, we must recognize Christ in the poorest, his brethren" (1397). This obligation relates directly to the nature of the human person (especially the innate quality of being in relation to others) and the principle of solidarity. It has important consequences for one's relationship with God. "God blesses those who come to the aid of the poor and rebukes those who turn away from them" (2443).

The love of the poor required by the Gospel directly relates to the manner in which the goods of the earth are regarded and used. "Love of the poor is incompatible with immoderate love of riches or their selfish use" (2445). Moreover, the duty to share goods with the poor is considered not to be merely a work of mercy, but rather to be a requirement of justice. "Not to enable the poor to share in our goods is to steal from them and deprive them of life. The goods we possess are not ours, but theirs" (St. John Chrysostom, quoted in 2446). The poverty that is the focus of this love is not just material, but is also cultural and religious poverty as well (2444). Everyone thus bears a serious personal obligation to care for the poor and to take their needs into account in deciding on the use of material goods.

It is worth noting that the *Catechism* condemns "*immoderate* love of riches and their *selfish* use" (2445, emphasis added). There is no support in the *Catechism* for the uncritical view that riches are immoral *per se*. The teachings of the Church do not establish the moral inferiority — or superiority — of wealth. As with any endowment, natural or obtained, the key to moral conduct is in the use made of it (see, e.g., Mt 25:14-46).

Translating these principles into social policy is a matter of considerable contention. The teachings of the Church do not mandate any particular legislative approaches. However, the laws of any community, especially any relief measures, must embody a genuine love for the poor. But they must also serve the common good of all members of society and respect fundamental rights. So, for instance, confiscatory taxes or coercive land distribution plans would be unjust, despite their source in a genuine concern for the poor. Such policies violate the natural right to the possession and use of private property, and would certainly damage the economic health of society (and thus the common good). Illustrations of these policies can be found in the history of any number of socialist and Communist states, where the ostensible justification for confiscating private property without just compensation has been the perceived interests of the proletariat or peasantry. Such government acts are indistinguishable from outright theft, regardless of the laudable motive to end inequality and suffering in society. In addition, Pope John Paul II has expressed reservations about an overly bureaucratic approach to poverty relief that gives to central governments the duties and roles that should rest in the hands of intermediate institutions or associations, and ultimately the family (see *Centesimus Annus*, 48-49).

On the other hand, the needs of the poor cannot be sacrificed to the interests of other elements in society under the guise of serving the common good. The policies of the government of Great Britain during the great famine in Ireland in the 1840's would be an example. The blight that harmed the potato crop, of course, was the result of the forces of nature and was not morally attributable to anyone. However, the response by the civil authorities to the human misery caused by the crop failures certainly required a morally accountable response. Yet while multitudes starved or fled the country, the British government spent its best energies guarding food exports that were needed to feed its own urban workers, and offered merely perfunctory relief efforts. Intervening directly to relieve the effects of the famine was considered to be improper interference in the economy. In so doing, the government sacrificed the interests of the poor and suffering to ensure the well-being of others. This "acceptance... of murderous famine " was certainly "a grave offense" and utterly contrary to the common good and the moral law (2269).

In short, each government initiative that has an impact on the poor must be evaluated to see if it embodies the duty of love imposed by the Gospel, if it comports with the principles of solidarity and subsidiarity, and if it is consistent with social justice and the common good. Indeed, in formulating social policy, it is crucial to recognize that serving the best interests of the poor is a fundamental component of the common good.

The "universal destination of goods" also has implications for the international community. The world is faced with great inequalities of resources and economic capability between nations (2437). This inequality is reflected in "usurious financial systems, iniquitous commercial relations among nations, and the arms race" (2438). The just social order on the international level would replace these "perverse mechanisms" with a sense of solidarity between nations, and "a common effort to mobilize resources toward objectives of moral, cultural, and economic development" (2438).

Rich nations have a particularly "grave moral responsibility" to poorer nations, out of solidarity and charity (2439). It is also a duty of justice in those cases where the wealth of rich nations has come from exploitative economic arrangements (2439). Such would be the case with those nations that have pursued mercantilist methods of colonization, where the resources of the colony were developed solely towards the benefit of the mother country without regard to the good of the people of the colony. Once these colonies were liberated, they were left in a very unfavorable posture. Either they continued to be dependent on their former master (or transnational corporations), or they struggled with unbalanced economies that were unable to provide sufficient prosperity to their people and to compete in the world market. As a result, many developing countries have fallen under the thrall of crushing national debts. Examples of this abound in the history of Africa and South America, and have led to many calls for forgiving these debts as part of a biblically-modeled millennial "Jubilee" (see the many expressions of support for debt reduction or forgiveness by Pope John Paul II, e.g., in *Tertio Millennio Adveniente*, 51, and statements by many national bishops' conferences).

Especially since the Second Vatican Council, the Church has spoken out strongly for development in the poorer areas of the world (see, e.g., *Populorum Progressio* and *Sollicitudo Rei Socialis*). This development can be the fruit of direct aid to governments or individuals, or in the form of broader reforms of international financial institutions, "so that they will better promote equitable relationships with less advanced countries" (2440). The efforts of less-developed countries themselves are to be supported, especially in the area of agrarian reform, given the large number of peasants among the poor of the world (2440).

The weak record of some international development efforts gives cause for caution in evaluating specific applications of these ideals. Certainly, the principle of subsidiarity should be applied to all aid initiatives. It would favor such programs as Catholic Relief Services, which works closely with individuals and communities to enhance self-sufficiency, rather than through governmental structures. This is especially important in light of the oppressiveness, rampant corruption and inefficiency of governments in many nations.

Development efforts must also not lend support to the violation of fundamental rights. For example, in recent years, the notion of international development has been heavily freighted with an ideology of population control that seeks to limit the size of families, particularly in less-developed countries. While the Church certainly recognizes that responsible parenthood involves social obligations, the need for development cannot justify cooperating in unjust population control policies (such as the repugnant policy of coercive family planning and forced abortions imposed by the governments, or policies that condition international aid on the distribution of contraceptives or the legalization of abortion). Indeed, social policies that intrude upon the freedom of a husband and wife to make free decisions about the size of their family are gravely unjust (see *Charter of the Rights of the Family*, Article 3).

In addition, an excessive emphasis on demographics, which is merely one aspect of genuine development, can certainly divert attention from other, more essential needs. For instance, the Church is careful to stress that development is not solely an economic phenomenon. Instead, it must involve the progress of the entire human person. "True development concerns the whole man. It is concerned with increasing each person's ability to respond to his vocation and hence to God's call" (2461).

Humanity's obligation to be a steward of the goods of creation also affects policies towards the environment. Natural resources (including animals and plants) "are by nature destined for the common good of past, present and future humanity"

45

(2415). Man does not enjoy absolute dominion over these resources, but is "limited by concern for the quality of life of his neighbor, including generations to come," and must have "a religious respect for the integrity of creation" (2415). Therefore, society must include a concern for the stewardship of nature in its calculus of the common good.

J. ECONOMIC ACTIVITY IS A RIGHT AND OBLIGATION OF ALL MEMBERS OF SOCIETY, AND IS DEDICATED TO THE SERVICE OF THE PERSON.

Every person has the fundamental right to economic initiative, and "should make legitimate use of his talents to contribute to the abundance that will benefit all and to harvest the just fruits of his labor" (2429). In pursuit of their economic activities, people have the right to own and use private property (2403). This activity, however, must be centered on the proper goals, and carried out in the proper manner:

> The development of economic activity and growth in production are meant to provide for the needs of human beings. Economic life is not meant solely to multiply goods produced and increase profit or power; it is ordered first of all to the service of persons, of the whole man, and of the entire human community. (2426)

In the economic realm, a proper respect for the dignity of the human person requires that certain virtues be practiced: temperance, so that one does not become unduly attached to material goods; justice, to ensure that all receive their due; and solidarity, to reflect the example of Jesus (2407). Economic initiatives must be conducted pursuant to the requirements of the moral order, "in keeping with social justice so as to correspond to God's plan for man" (2426). As a result, all those involved in the economy bear certain responsibilities.

All parties to economic disputes are obligated to resolve their differences peacefully. This derives directly from the duty to serve the common good, and to act with a spirit of solidarity. The Church recognizes that in the economic realm, there will necessarily be competing — even conflicting — interests within society, such as business owners/employers, wage earners, and the public authorities. Any conflicts that arise from this competition should be resolved by negotiation, in a manner that protects the rights and duties of all (2430). All economic actors "should also seek to observe regulations issued by legitimate authority for the sake of the common good" (2429).

Society as a whole is required to guarantee that conditions exist for every person to fulfill the right to economic initiative. This "presupposes sure guarantees of individual freedom and private property, as well as a stable currency and efficient public services" (*Centesimus Annus*, 48). It is the principal task of the state to ensure this level of security, "so that those who work and produce can enjoy the fruits of their labors and thus feel encouraged to work efficiently and honestly" (*Centesimus Annus*, 48). The state must also oversee the exercise of human rights, help citizens find work and employment, and to require the payment of social security contributions (2431, 2436).

Business owners and employers have a number of rights and obligations in the economic order. In conducting their businesses, they are obliged "to consider the good of persons and not only the increase of profits" (2432). Contrary to a widely-held but erroneous belief, the Church is not hostile to the profit motive. "Profits are necessary.... They make possible the investments that ensure the future of a business and they guarantee employment" (2432). This merely recognizes a basic reality of market economies — the private sector must be the engine of economic prosperity and employment, and to do so it must be free to pursue profits. In addition, businesses must bear in mind that they are "responsible to society for the economic and ecological effects of their operations" (2432).

With regard to employment, there are specific duties for businesses. "Access to employment and to professions must be open to all without unjust discrimination: men and women, healthy and disabled, natives and immigrants" (2433). Business enterprises are also strictly enjoined to pay their workers a just wage. "To refuse or withhold it can be a grave injustice" (2434). In determining what is just, the needs and contribution of workers must both be taken into account. One's pay should "guarantee man the opportunity to provide a dignified livelihood for himself and his family on the material, social, cultural, and spiritual level, taking into account the role and the productivity of each, the state of the business, and the common good" (*Gaudium et Spes*, 67). In determining the just rate of pay, the Church specifically condemns the notion of the unregulated market for wages — "Agreement between the parties is not sufficient to justify morally the amount to be received in wages" (2434).

One need only look to the history of the mining industry in the United States to see a classic illustration of the abuse of workers by businesses that acted in a manner entirely unrestrained by moral principle. In many areas (e.g., the coal fields of Appalachia), wealthy and politically powerful mining companies enjoyed a surplus of potential workers, ineffective or nonexistent labor laws, and legal barriers to unionization. They were also abetted by corrupt and subservient governments, who failed to offer even minimal protection to workers seeking to vindicate their civil and natural rights. Many companies, and some governments, were actively involved in the violent repression of workers. Efforts to organize unions frequently were met with extra-judicial executions and brutal repression. These businesses justified their exploitation of their workers by appealing to the principle of "freedom of contract" in the setting of wages and work conditions — ignoring the fact that the individual miners were powerless to negotiate from a position of equal strength. These manifest wrongs were abhorrent to the natural law and the principle of solidarity. Indeed, injustice to the wage earner has been specifically condemned by Sacred Scripture as one of the "sins that cry to heaven" (1867, citing Dt 24:14-15 and Jm 5:4).

Workers themselves have rights and responsibilities in the economy. Most fundamentally, work is a duty — "If anyone will not work, let him not eat" (2 Th 3:10, cited in 2427). People must take charge of their own economic situation by "conscientious work" (1914). Parents in particular are obliged "to provide as far as possible for the physical... needs of their children" (2252). The principle of subsidiarity mandates that primary responsibility in the economic sphere really falls upon individuals, rather than the state, and upon intermediary groups (2431).

The principles of solidarity and subsidiarity necessarily involve the right to form labor unions. "Among the basic rights of the human person is to be numbered the right of freely founding unions for working people. These should be able truly to represent them and to contribute to the organizing of economic life in the right way. Included is the right of freely taking part in the activity of these unions without risk of reprisal" (*Gaudium et Spes,* 68). This "natural human right" has been consistently proclaimed and defended by the Church throughout the last century (see, e.g., *Rerum Novarum*, 48 ff., and *Centesimus Annus*, 7), and is implicit in the *Catechism* (see, e.g., 2430). Workers have the right to strike "when it cannot be avoided, or at least when it is necessary to obtain a proportionate benefit" (2435). In exercising that right, violence cannot be used, nor can goals be sought that "are not directly linked to working conditions or are contrary to the common good" (2435). Inspired by the social teachings of the Church to vindicate these basic human rights, brave men and women embarked in 1980 on one of history's most heroic enterprises — the Solidarity labor movement in Poland. It should not be a surprise that Pope John Paul II, a former archbishop of Krakow and a major supporter of Solidarity, has been an indefatigable defender and promoter of the interests of workers (see, e.g., his encyclical on human work, *Laborem Exercens*).

Note that the Church's understanding of economic activity and the relations between actors in the marketplace is at sharp variance with certain theories of liberal economics. In the latter view, people are primarily viewed as individual economic agents, making rational decisions in the market according to their calculus of their own interest. With this dominant economic motivation, people are linked with each other only by choice, through the formation of contractual relationships of more or less permanency. In contrast, the Church's view stems from the inherently relational nature of humanity and our supernatural destiny. Instead of being an isolated individual in the market, each person is a participant in a web of economic and social relationships. We make decisions in our own economic interest, to be sure, but these decisions must always be tempered by a concern for our immortal soul, the strength of our family, the concerns of the community (subsidiarity), the needs of our fellows (solidarity and social justice) and the well-being of society as a whole (the common good).

In addition to the rights and responsibilities of individuals, the *Catechism* examines the moral implications of the great socio-economic systems that have dominated modern times.

The Church takes as her premise that "Any system in which social relationships are determined entirely by economic factors is contrary to the nature of the human person and his acts" (2423). This is directly derived from the Catholic understanding that the human person is not an exclusively material being, but is spiritual as well, and that his life is ordered to the development of his relationship with God, rather than just to material well-being. From this follows the judgment that "A theory that makes profit the exclusive norm and ultimate end of economic activity is morally unacceptable" (2424).

Casting her eyes about the world today, and back across history, the Church understands that "the disordered desire for money" has had significant deleterious consequences for society, including causing "many conflicts which disturb the social order" (2424). The *Catechism* echoes the words of Christ in warning that "Every practice that reduces persons to nothing more than a means of profit enslaves man, leads to idolizing money, and contributes to the spread of atheism: 'You cannot serve God and mammon'" (2424, quoting Mt 6:24). The Church has "refused to accept, in the practice of 'capitalism,' individualism and the absolute primacy of the law of the marketplace over human labor... Regulating [the economy] solely by the law of the marketplace fails social justice, for 'there are many human needs which cannot be satisfied by the market'" (2425, quoting *Centesimus Annus*, 34).

This should stand as a sobering rebuke to certain theories

of economics prevalent in the market economies of the West. Particularly in legal and political circles, there is a strain of thinking that focuses almost exclusively on an economic analysis of public affairs and of human behavior, and that favors a virtually unrestricted market economy as the best (and most free) form of social and economic organization. This runs a substantial risk of reducing one's concept of the person to that of a fungible object and a radically free agent in an impersonal economic "system" or "market." To do so would diminish the sense of solidarity that each person must have for his fellows, and ultimately would lead to the degradation of human dignity. It also is rooted in a strict materialism that either denies, or is indifferent to, humanity's spiritual nature and our moral responsibility for the use of freedom.

The Church does not reserve her fire for Western economic theories. "Collectivism" as a method of social organization is specifically rejected (1885). Likewise, the *Catechism* condemns "the totalitarian and atheistic ideologies associated in modern times with 'communism' or 'socialism'" (2425). It goes on to observe that "Regulating the economy solely by centralized planning perverts the basis of social bonds..." (2425).

Opposition to Marxism has certainly been a hallmark of Catholic social teaching over the last century. This has stemmed from Communism's atheism and materialism, its aggressive and violent attempts to spread "revolution" to other countries, and the brutal tyranny (including but not limited to the suppression of religious freedom) that has accompanied it everywhere on the globe. Indeed, the heart of *Centesimus Annus*, which was issued by Pope John Paul II in 1991, is a powerful reflection on the meaning of the peaceful revolutions of 1989 that overthrew the Communist yoke on Eastern Europe. John Paul concluded that the failure of socialism resulted from its flawed understanding of human nature, its instrumental view of the human person as an economic actor, and its refusal to acknowledge that genuine freedom entails the moral choice between good and evil. Ironically, these failings are also found in large measure in the consumer mentality that has engulfed the West and threatens the formerly-Communist and the developing nations. As Pope John Paul stated:

> [T]he fundamental error of socialism is anthropological in nature. Socialism considers the individual person as an element, a molecule within the social organism, so that the good of the individual is completely subordinated to the functioning of the socioeconomic mechanism. Socialism likewise maintains that the good of the individual can be realized without reference to his free choice, to the unique and exclusive responsibility he exercises in the face of good or evil. Man is thus reduced to a series of social relationships, and the concept of the person as the autonomous subject of moral decision disappears... (*Centesimus Annus*, 13).

The teachings of the Church on the great socio-economic systems are not just critical, but also prescriptive. The strong defense of private property and the fundamental right of individual economic initiative, together with the condemnation of collectivism, makes clear that the *Catechism* favors free market economies — what is commonly called "capitalism." The market, however, cannot be unrestrained — "Reasonable regulation of the marketplace and economic initiatives, in keeping with a just hierarchy of values and a view to the common good, is to be commended" (2425). Pope John Paul II is very clear on this question:

Can it perhaps be said that after the failure of communism capitalism is the victorious social system and that capitalism should be the goal of the countries now making efforts to rebuild their economy and society? Is this the model which ought to be proposed to the countries of the Third World which are searching for the path to true economic and civil progress? The answer is obviously complex. If by "capitalism" is meant an economic system which recognizes the fundamental and positive role of business, the market, private property, and the resulting responsibility for the means of production as well as free human creativity in the economic sector, then the answer is certainly in the affirmative, even though it would perhaps be more appropriate to speak of a "business economy," "market economy," or simply "free economy." But if by "capitalism" is meant a system in which freedom in the economic sector is not circumscribed within a strong juridical framework which places it at the service of human freedom in its totality and which sees it as a particular aspect of that freedom, the core of which is ethical and religious, then the reply is certainly negative. (*Centesimus Annus*, 42)

It is important to note the qualifications in John Paul's endorsement of the "market economy." Nevertheless, the Church's moral judgment has clearly agreed with the results of history, rejecting Marxism and its manifestations in favor of the regulated but free economies of the West.

K. SOCIETY AND ALL CITIZENS HAVE AN OBLIGATION TO SEEK AND PRESERVE PEACE.

In the Gospels, Our Lord Jesus Christ enjoins us to reject violence and hatred, and to embrace peace of heart. This commandment of love extends even towards one's enemies (2302 ff.; see, e.g., Lk 6:27-35). These principles, together with the obligation to respect human life, require peace in society (2304).

"Peace is not merely the absence of war" (2304). It entails more than maintaining a balance of power between potential adversaries, but the positive promotion of virtues inherent in the common good and social justice: "safeguarding the goods of persons, free communication among men, respect for the dignity of persons and peoples, and the assiduous practice of fraternity" (2304). It is thus "'the tranquility of order'... the work of justice and the effect of charity" (2304). True peace cannot be attained by human efforts alone. Instead, it consists of "the peace of Christ," the reconciliation between God and humanity wrought by "the blood of his Cross" (2305).

The Church imposes upon all citizens and governments the duty to work for the prevention of war through prayer and action (2307, 2308). Pacifism — the renunciation of violence — is valued and respected, so long as it does not harm "the rights and obligations of other men and societies" (2306). The Church recognizes, however, that in a world "inundated by sin" (401, 2317), the danger of war will persist. Therefore, nations are permitted "the right of lawful self-defense, once all peace efforts have failed" (*Gaudium et Spes*, 79). Indeed, it is a basic duty of civil authorities to protect the community from aggression (2266). To that end, the state may impose obligations on its citizens that are necessary for the defense of the nation (2308).

When the state exercises its right to use military force, a rigorous moral analysis must be pursued by those responsible for safeguarding the common good (2309). This involves the application of what has traditionally been referred to as the "just war" doctrine:

- "the damage inflicted by the aggressor on the nation or community of nations must be lasting, grave, and certain;
- all other means of putting an end to it must have been shown to be impractical or ineffective;
- there must be serious prospects of success;
- the use of arms must not produce evils and disorders graver than the evil to be eliminated. The power of modern means of destruction weighs very heavily in evaluating this condition" (2309).

These principles can be applied to concrete historical examples. There are a myriad of patently unjust wars in human history. In our own century, they would include the German invasion of Belgium and France in 1914, the Nazi aggressions of World War II, the Japanese attack on Pearl Harbor, the North Korean invasion of South Korea in 1950, the Syrian and Egyptian attack against Israel in the Yom Kippur War of 1973, and many others. There have also been a number of clearly justified uses of military force. Instances would include the opposition to the above-cited unjust aggressions, as well as Operation Desert Storm in 1991. Other international conflicts are morally ambiguous, such as the Six-Day War of 1967. Common factors that unite the just wars are that they have been primarily defensive in nature, or have been dedicated to expelling an unjust aggressor.

In applying a moral analysis to armed conflict, it is crucial to distinguish between the justification for use of military force and the way in which it is used. A war that was morally justifiable can be prosecuted in a morally unacceptable manner. "The Church and human reason both assert the permanent validity of the moral law during armed conflict. 'The mere fact that war has regrettably broken out does not mean that everything becomes licit between the warring parties'" (2312, quoting *Gaudium et Spes*, 79). Indeed, the need for "rules of war" has been recognized by international society in the adoption of a series of agreements known as the Geneva Conventions relating to the treatment of non-combatants, prisoners, and the methods and weapons of war.

In particular, the Church has strongly stated that "the extermination of a people, nation, or ethnic minority must be condemned as a mortal sin. One is morally bound to resist orders that command genocide" (2313). The Church likewise condemns "every act of war directed to the indiscriminate destruction of whole cities or vast areas with their inhabitants" as "a crime against God and man" (*Gaudium et Spes*, 80). Indeed, "a danger of modern warfare is that it provides the opportunity to those who possess modern scientific weapons — especially atomic, biological, or chemical weapons — to commit such crimes" (2314).

The general acceptance of these rules can be seen in the war crimes trials after World War II, in which barbaric conduct by German and Japanese soldiers and government officials were condemned, and in attempts to proscribe the crimes committed during "ethnic cleansing" in the former Yugoslav republics. Other examples of unjustified acts during wartime abound, such as the use of poison gas in World War I, the carpet bombing and fire bombing of cities by all sides in World War II, barbaric medical experiments on prisoners by Nazis and Japanese doctors during World War II, and the torture of prisoners by the Chinese in the Korean War and by the North Vietnamese in the Vietnam War.

The accumulation of armaments, particularly in the context of the "arms race" and international sales of weapons, also raise substantial moral questions. Throughout history, the maintenance of a balance of power between competing nations has been seen as a very effective way to preserve peace. The underlying assumption has been to deter aggression by convincing one's adversaries that the cost of initiating warfare would be prohibitive, and its chance of success low. A prominent example can be found in the military strategy of the Western allies and the Soviet bloc during the Cold War. In an effort to deter conventional or nuclear aggression, the superpowers pursued the theory of "mutually assured destruction." This meant that each side would maintain sufficient nuclear arms to survive any first strike (even if it otherwise destroyed their nation), and would use those arms to assure the utter devastation of their enemy. The intent was to convince the other side that launching aggression would be futile, because it would inevitably result in their own annihilation. This effort necessarily entailed the expenditure of enormous sums of money and energy, as both sides sought to ensure that their arsenals were technologically advanced and sizeable enough to survive a first strike and effect massive retaliation — hence the term "arms race."

Even though it can be argued that this strategy actually deters aggression, the Church nevertheless declares it to be morally unacceptable. "The arms race does not ensure peace. Far from eliminating the causes of war, it risks aggravating them.... Over-armament multiplies reasons for conflict and increases the danger of escalation" (2315). The wisdom of this

judgment can be seen in the history of Western Europe leading to World War I, where vigorously competing alliances and
a virtually unrestrained arms race led to a sense that war was
inevitable — as well as both necessary and desirable — to resolve international tensions and underlying rivalries. The out-
break of war, and the terrible destruction it produced, certainly
resulted from these factors.

Moreover, the use of precious resources in purchasing
weapons of destruction has significant social cost, especially in
less-developed areas of the world. The massive expenditure of
money on arms "impedes efforts to aid needy populations; it
thwarts the development of peoples" (2315). The international
arms trade, if left unregulated, certainly contributes to insta-
bility and tension that may lead to conflict (2316). "The arms
race is one of the greatest curses on the human race and the
harm it inflicts on the poor is more than can be endured"
(*Gaudium et Spes*, 81). In this context, it is worth recalling one
of the core principles of Christian moral doctrine: "one may not
do evil so that good may result from it" (1756).

In this area, the common good of all nations, and social
justice on the international level, would be best served by ad-
herence to the words of Jesus: "Blessed are the peacemakers,
for they shall be called sons of God" (Mt 5:9).

L. SOCIETY MUST STRENGTHEN AND PROTECT THE
    FAMILY.

The family is the foundation of every society. It is "the
original cell of social life" (2207). "This social institution is prior
to any recognition by public authority, which has an obligation
to recognize it" (2202). By definition, the family consists of a

husband and wife, united in a covenant of life and love, together with their children (2202, 2207). This definition of the family is to be "the normal reference point by which the different forms of family relationship are to be evaluated" (2202). The nature of the family and its basic constitution come directly from God from the time of creation — the family is a fundamental aspect of the divine plan for humanity (2203, 371 ff.).

The strength of every society reflects the strength of the families that comprise it. "Authority, stability, and a life of relationships within the family constitute the foundations for freedom, security and fraternity within society" (2207). Indeed, nobody who regards the deterioration of Western society can fail to recognize that it stems from and is largely determined by a decline in the health of families. This stands to reason. "The family is the community in which, from childhood, one can learn moral values, begin to honor God, and make good use of freedom. Family life is an initiation into life in society" (2207). If there are problems in the lives of families, there will be a resulting failure to inculcate morality, piety, and responsible freedom. The effects of this certainly have a negative impact on society.

Each family is obligated to conduct their communal lives in a way that reflects responsibility towards, and solidarity with, other members of society. "The family should live in such a way that its members learn to care and take responsibility for the young, the old, the sick, the handicapped, and the poor" (2208). This duty is at the heart of the Church's notion of subsidiarity (2208). In addition, the nature of the family teaches and enhances our understanding of human solidarity. "The home is the natural environment for initiating a human being into solidarity and communal responsibilities" (2224).

"The importance of the family for the life and well-being

of society entails a particular responsibility for society to support and strengthen marriage and the family" (2210). Society must guarantee the rights of families, including:

- The right to establish a family, have children, and educate them in keeping with the family's traditions, cultural values, and moral and religious beliefs;
- The right to stability of the bond of marriage and of the institution of the family;
- The right to believe in and profess one's faith and to propagate it;
- The right to have adequate means to support one's family, to own private property, to engage in free economic activity, to obtain medical care and adequate housing, and to emigrate;
- The right, especially of the poor and the sick, to obtain physical, social, political and economic security;
- The right to form associations with other families, and to have representation before civil authorities;
- The right to protection of physical and moral health, especially from the dangers of drugs, pornography, alcoholism, etc. (see *Familiaris Consortio*, 46; cf. 2211).

Through these specific applications of her social teaching, the Church demonstrates that she is staunchly pro-family. It is worth noting that these policies emphasize the duty of the state to enable families to achieve moral and spiritual development, as well as to assist in their material well-being. It is also important to observe that the principle of subsidiarity is central to this approach.

There is often much talk in the American political arena about "family values." It is often used as a partisan incantation, or as a slogan for the affirmation of traditional moral values. One must not permit this usage to divest the term of its value (as is often the case in politics, where words lose their genuine meaning or are twisted until they become unrecognizable). Nor should it be allowed to become yet another political code word, whose sole purpose is to manipulate or demonize various constituencies. This is by no means an exclusively modern phenomenon. In describing the corrosive effect of politics (specifically a civil war) on the use of language, the ancient historian Thucydides perceptively observed, "To fit in with the change of events, words, too, had to change their usual meanings."

There is a dire need for society to take seriously its obligation to protect and strengthen the family in the face of the myriad threats unleashed by modern culture. The agenda proposed by the Church would offer a sound basis for the support and development of strong families. Specific applications of these principles might include ensuring that marriage is given a privileged place in the law (e.g., through favorable treatment in tax codes), mandating parental involvement in important aspects of their children's lives (e.g., education and health care), restricting free divorce (especially when there are children from the union), and discouraging cohabitation outside of marriage or other non-marital arrangements (e.g., by refusing recognition to so-called "domestic partnerships," or by restructuring public assistance regulations that create disincentives to marriage).

In order to advance the genuine development of all, to vouchsafe the common good, and to ensure social justice, society must look constantly to the health of its families. As Pope John Paul II has said, "A family policy must be the basis and driving force of all social policies" (*Evangelium Vitae*, 90). The vigorous promotion and defense of the family has been a hallmark of the pontificate of John Paul II. See *Familiaris Consortio* (especially 46), *The Letter to Families* (especially 17), and *The Charter of the Rights of the Family* (a comprehensive statement of family rights issued by the Holy See in 1983).

M. RELIGIOUS BELIEF HAS A PRIVILEGED ROLE IN THE LIFE OF SOCIETY.

It is an inherent part of human nature to seek the truth, especially the truth that pertains to God (2104, 2467). This stems from "the very dignity of the human person," which seeks to know and understand its Creator, to whom its entire life is ordered (*Dignitatis Humanae*, 2, quoted in 2104). Once men discover the truth, they are bound to adhere to it, and to direct their entire lives, and all their acts, in accordance with it (2467).

The innate orientation of humanity to religious truth is a fundamental component of human freedom. "The right to the exercise of freedom, especially in moral and religious matters, is an inalienable requirement of the dignity of the human person" (1738). Society must respect the liberty of men to enjoy freedom of conscience, without any state coercion (1738). This guarantees that "nobody may be forced to act against his conscience, nor is anyone to be restrained from acting in accordance with his conscience in religious matters in private or in public, alone or in association with others" (*Dignitatis Humanae*, 2, quoted in 2106). The *Catechism* takes care to note, however, that freedom of conscience is not freedom to engage in moral license or to adhere to error (2108). "The exercise of freedom does not imply a right to say or do everything... By deviating from the moral law man violates his own freedom, becomes imprisoned within himself, disrupts neighborly fellowship, and rebels against divine truth" (1740; see also *Veritatis Splendor, passim*).

Freedom of religious conscience is a significant limit on state authority, and it is a necessary component of the common good (1907). It is a hallmark of free societies to permit wide latitude in the expression of religious belief. This is reflected in legal provisions such as the First Amendment to the United States Constitution and the provisions of the Universal Declaration of Human Rights, which guarantee religious liberty to all. Likewise, it is characteristic of oppressive regimes that they seek to restrict religious worship and expression, recognizing that the freedom of humanity to seek the truth is always a threat to tyrants.

Perhaps the best example of the power of religion to foster human freedom can be seen in the role played by the Church, along with other religious communities and people of faith, in the bloodless revolutions that toppled the Communist regimes in Eastern Europe in 1989. More recently, in 1997, there were reports that the government of Vietnam, one of the few remaining Communist dictatorships, blocked publication of the *Catechism* unless the entire Part III ("Life in Christ") were omitted. Since this section contains the moral teaching of the Church, including the social doctrine and the teaching on the dignity of the human person, this episode demonstrates once again that the gravest threat to a tyranny is the truth. Despots everywhere fear religion, because it calls men to the truth, and thus to liberty.

This essential freedom, however, also brings with it a correlative duty to follow the dictates of one's religious beliefs. This has profound social significance. "The social duty of Christians is to respect and awaken in each person the love of the true and the good" (2105). It is part of the evangelization of the Church to enable men "to infuse the Christian spirit into the mentality and mores, laws and structures of the communities in which [they] live" (*Apostolicam Actuositatem*, 13). Men are thus called and empowered to promote "a continually renewed conversion of the social partners" based on their Christian faith (1916).

In this regard, the Church has an important function. The Church challenges the political authorities of every society and in every age to measure their acts against the revealed truth about God and humanity (2244). This does not mean that there should be a merger of the functions of the Church and the state, or that an established church is mandated by Catholic doctrine. Such constitutional arrangements, which have been common in history and continue to be a reality in some countries, raise significant concerns for the religious freedom of individuals (2107; see also *Dignitatis Humanae, passim*).

The "separation of Church and state" actually serves to liberate the Church from political control and interference, freeing it to perform its genuine function. "The Church… is not to be confused in any way with the political community" (2245). Rather, part of the Church's mission is "to pass moral judgments even in matters related to politics, whenever the fundamental rights of man or the salvation of souls requires it" (*Gaudium et Spes*, 76).

This role of the Church is an essential safeguard for human liberty and happiness. Many societies have failed to recognize humanity's origin and destiny in God, along with the reality of standards of objective good and evil. These societies "arrogate to themselves an explicit or implicit totalitarian power over man and his destiny" (2244). The danger of totalitarianism is not limited to socialist or fascist regimes. Pope John Paul

II has noted that liberal democracies can impose a paradoxical form of totalitarianism through the naked power of popular majorities that do not recognize the truth and fail to conform to it (see *Evangelium Vitae*, 20).

Within the Church, it is primarily the task of the laity to bring religious values to bear on social concerns. "By reason of their special vocation it belongs to the laity to seek the kingdom of God by engaging in temporal affairs and directing them according to God's will" (*Lumen Gentium*, 31). It is particularly for lay Christians to discover and invent "the means for permeating social, political, and economic realities with the demands of Christian doctrine and life" (899). This includes reforming institutions and conditions that are an "inducement to sin," and ensuring that they "may be conformed to the norms of justice, favoring rather than hindering the practice of virtue. By doing so, they will impregnate culture and human works with a moral value" (*Lumen Gentium*, 36).

Many people are uncomfortable with the idea of religious belief having an influence on public affairs. Contemporary Americans have been nurtured in a culture that is suspicious of — and frequently hostile to — religious expression outside of the sphere of private belief and conduct. Many Americans give talismanic significance to the so-called "wall of separation" between church and state, to use Thomas Jefferson's phrase. In this view, the affairs of the secular world are outside the jurisdiction of faith, and should be immune to its influence. Such an attitude relegates religion to the sidelines (and to a second-class status) while the ordering of society is determined by other standards, such as economics or class theory. This is one of the more corrosive legacies of the Enlightenment's hostility to revealed truth and authority in general. It has embroiled humanity in a struggle that recognizes no objective truths, only competing interests. The result is that debates about social concerns can be resolved only through the exercise of raw political power. As the recent history of the United States demonstrates, this does not foster the necessary sense of solidarity in society, and seriously undermines peace and mutual respect.

Catholic social thought makes manifest that the health of society and the well-being of all people depend on the recognition of humanity's proper relation to God, and the ordering of society according to the divine will. As the Fathers of the Second Vatican Council declared,

> [I]n every temporal affair [the faithful] are to be guided by a Christian conscience, since no human activity, even of the temporal order, can be withdrawn from God's dominion (*Lumen Gentium*, 36).

Conclusion

A s we have seen, Catholic social teaching presents a comprehensive approach to the ordering of society, and the
relationship between humanity and God. As such, it offers a
body of doctrine, a system of thought, and a model for behavior. It is, however, not just an alternative socio-political philosophy. Rather, it is an intrinsic part of the life of the Church,
and most particularly a fundamental part of the vocation of the
laity.

By virtue of their Baptism and Confirmation, and empowered by the graces received through the Eucharist, the laity are
called to be "sharers in their particular way in the priestly, pro-
phetic, and kingly office of Christ" (897). Through their actions
in the world, the laity participate in the priestly office by
"consecrat[ing] the world itself to God" (901). They are proph-
ets by witnessing to their faith and by evangelizing "in the or-
dinary circumstances of the world" (905). And they take part
in Christ's kingship by remedying social conditions and structures that serve as inducements to sin, by promoting justice,
and by acting to "impregnate culture and human works with a
moral value" (909).

In proclaiming the truth about humanity, society, and their
proper relationship with God, the Church works to prepare this
sinful world for the Kingdom of God. We pray for this every

day in Our Lord's own words. By working to transform the world in accordance with these teachings, we do not merely contribute to the progress of society and culture. We do much more. We join our voices in the fervent prayer that is the culmination of the New Testament, a prayer that embodies our yearning for the reign of true peace, justice, and grace: "Come, Lord Jesus!"

Some Questions and Problems Raised by the Application of Catholic Social Teaching

Whenever the social teaching of the Church moves from the realm of principle into concrete applications, some significant questions inevitably arise. A brief discussion of some of these concerns would be useful to an understanding of the Church's social doctrine, especially since many of them relate to the authority of papal and episcopal pronouncements, as well as the relative competence of the laity and clergy in making pragmatic judgments about political and social policies.

Whenever individual bishops or a bishops' conference speak out on social issues, they face two difficult and related questions: the authority of the statement, and the proper role and response by the laity. The Code of Canon Law states the general principle that when the bishops exercise their teaching authority, either as individuals or through a collective body like a national conference, "the faithful must adhere to the authentic teaching of their own bishops with a sense of religious respect" (Can. 753). Likewise, the *Catechism* calls to mind the authority of the Church as carrying on the teaching of Christ

Himself, and says that "the faithful receive with docility the teachings and directives that their pastors give them in various forms" (87). At the same time, the vocation of the laity involves action in the social sphere in order to implement the Gospel. "The initiative of lay Christians is necessary especially when the matter involves discovering or inventing the means for permeating social, political, and economic realities with the demands of Christian doctrine and life" (899).

While these principles are certainly not incompatible, they may involve some tension. For instance, in applying Catholic social teaching to particular issues, the bishops must be careful not to propose a prudential judgment as a definitive moral teaching. In addition, the bishops and laity must both be attentive to the risk of scandal if controversial statements on social issues result in open dissent from underlying doctrinal or moral principles. At the same time, given the complexity of many social issues, there is a risk of eroding the credibility of Church teaching authority with pronouncements on issues that require particular expertise, for instance in economic matters. Nevertheless, the Church clearly cannot acquiesce in a tyranny of experts, in which only those who have the correct initials after their names are permitted to speak on certain subjects.

An example of the tension involved in these situations can be seen in the reaction to statements by the bishops on the death penalty. The teaching of the Church on this subject, as expressed in recent years in both the *Catechism* and in *Evangelium Vitae*, is essentially that the state has the authority to impose the death penalty if it is necessary to protect society against an "unjust aggressor"; however, if non-lethal means are available to ensure society's safety, these methods should be used instead (2267). Moreover, reflecting the pastoral judgment of Pope John Paul II, the *Catechism* goes on to state that in the present circumstances, "the cases in which the execution of the offender is an absolute necessity 'are very rare, if not practically non-existent'" (2267, quoting *Evangelium Vitae*, 56). Even before these two documents, many American bishops, either individually or through the national or state conferences, have expressed their own pastoral judgment that capital punishment is unnecessary and should be avoided (see, e.g., "U.S. Bishops' Statement on Capital Punishment," November 1980).

The reaction of the laity to these pronouncements is very instructive. Many have welcomed the Church's intervention on this critical moral-political issue. However, some have argued that the Church has not gone far enough, and have openly dissented from the *Catechism*'s nuanced approval of capital punishment. Some have even alleged that this teaching undermines the Church's commitment to a "consistent ethic of life," and has thereby weakened its opposition to other threats to life, such as abortion or euthanasia. Other sincere Catholics disagree with the bishops' judgment about the need for the death penalty in order to reduce violent crime. Some have argued that since the bishops have no particular expertise in criminology, their statements should be given no more weight than the opinions of any other citizen. Indeed, some experts have pointedly disagreed with the bishops' arguments, particularly with the allegation that the death penalty is racially biased or that it has no deterrent effect.

Similar controversies have also resulted from two statements by the American bishops on the economy ("Economic Justice for All," November 1986) and national defense policy ("The Challenge of Peace," May 1983). In particular, these statements were met with strong criticism that the bishops had gone beyond their areas of expertise and had thereby undermined their own teaching authority.

The risk of scandal from dissent is particularly troubling. For instance, over the past few decades, the Church has repeatedly been faced with those who claim that it is an acceptable Catholic position to be "pro-choice" with regard to the legalization of abortion. The illegitimacy of this particular position has been made abundantly clear many times over (see, e.g., *Evangelium Vitae*, 71-74, and the United States bishops' statement "Living the Gospel of Life," November 1998), but it has proven to be vexing to the bishops and disconcerting to the faithful. It is very real concern that whenever a statement by the bishops engenders dissent (e.g., regarding the minimum wage, or farm policy), particularly when it is on a pragmatic issue that does not involve a core moral truth, there is a serious risk of confusing the faithful about the authority of pronouncements on more grave matters (e.g., the defense of human life). Clearly, the bishops must be prudent in balancing these concerns when they apply the social doctrine to specific issues.

Another problematic area is the accusation that the Church's statements on public policy issues represent improper "political" activity. Expressing an opinion on social issues is not necessarily a political act in the sense of showing a preference between competing parties. Of course, taking a stand on virtually any issue runs the risk of becoming entangled in "politics" in some sense, since it is the business of political parties to propose solutions to social problems, and the Church's position will inevitably tend to resemble that of one of the parties. Nevertheless, becoming too closely identified with any party could undermine the neutrality and credibility of the Church. This was the case in Western Europe in the nineteenth century, when the Church was widely perceived as being closely aligned with conservative forces against the growing industrial working class; this seriously impeded the Church's ability to retain the loyalty of many workers, and her ability to influence the labor movement. Here in the United States, some critics have derisively referred to the national bishops' conference as "the Democratic Party at prayer," due to the close identification between many of the bishops' positions and those of that party.

Some of the concern about "politics" stems from legitimate considerations about the relative roles of the hierarchy and the laity, and the proper role of the Church in society. Many people regard it as a serious infringement upon freedom of conscience for bishops to direct the faithful as to how to vote, either implicitly or explicitly. Others would prefer the bishops to be even more forceful, particularly in their explicit condemnation of "pro-choice" politicians, and would like to see the Church condemn anyone who votes for such a candidate. On the other hand, since Catholics in the United States still must deal with the stereotype that they are not loyal Americans or that they are beholden to a "foreign power," many would prefer that the bishops keep a low profile in the political arena, in order to avoid provoking a bigoted response. Some who oppose the Church's positions have even sought to intimidate her from becoming involved in the public debate, alleging that her actions violate the law against political activity by religious organizations. For example, in the 1980's the Church was the target of a lawsuit by abortion advocates who sought to have her tax-exempt status revoked, due to the bishops' advocacy against legalized abortion. Although the suit was ultimately defeated, it was costly and time-consuming to defend.

The need for prudence can be illustrated by a number of cases where the bishops have adopted a position that closely resembles the platform of a particular political party. For example, in their 1986 economic pastoral, the bishops of the United States tended to emphasize federal solutions to economic inequalities, based on a judgment that America's economic difficulties were a national concern that should be addressed by the federal government, rather than a matter that should be left primarily to experimentation and policy development by local and state officials, or to the operation of the free market. This approach resembled the general policy preferences of American liberals, and led many conservative advocates to suggest that the bishops were favoring the Democratic Party's positions. On the other hand, the bishops' strong opposition to abortion and euthanasia, and their support for taxpayer assistance to parents who send their children to private school, parallel the favored policies of conservatives, and have led some to accuse the Church of being too close to the Republican Party.

It is the nature of politicians of all faiths to seek political "cover" by citing their agreement with the Church's position, if it is in their best partisan interests. In such an environment, the bishops must tread warily, to avoid being co-opted by politicians. It is always worth recalling that whenever the Church has become too entangled with the state and with politics, the results have been disastrous for her in the long run, regardless of the short-term advantages. Leviathan is a difficult and unpredictable partner, and has an appetite that is hard to satiate.

Despite these legitimate concerns, it is nevertheless clear that the Church cannot remain silent on the practical applications of Catholic social doctrine. The bishops, as successors to the Apostles, have inherent competence — indeed, a specific charism — to teach the faithful and society as a whole about the nature of humanity and the proper ordering of the human community. The laity, likewise, share the responsibility to apply the Gospel to all aspects of life. Prudence, of course, is always needed. But so is courage.

Discussion Tips

There are many ways to apply Catholic social teaching to particular issues of the day. Indeed, there are very few issues for which the social doctrine can supply only one clear and indisputable policy recommendation. For instance, in a discussion of government fiscal and tax policies, one of the relevant principles of Catholic social teaching is the state's authority and duty to regulate the economy in a way that promotes the common good and social justice. However, there is likely to be a wide divergence of views about what constitutes the common good and social justice, and faithful Catholics may ardently disagree about how to accomplish those goals through legislation and regulation. Tax rates, the kinds and extent of available tax deductions and credits, the content and enforcement options for regulations, spending priorities, and other questions cannot be answered by looking at the *Catechism* or at papal encyclicals.

This does not in any way undermine the importance of the social doctrine in policy debates. The point is not for Catholic social teaching always to produce clear and unambiguous policy prescriptions. Instead, it is crucial to the good of society and mankind for individual Catholics and the Church as a whole to infuse policy debates with Gospel values, so that important social and political decisions are not made solely in the context of self-interest, factionalism, or political partisanship. Thus, while many may disagree about just what constitutes social justice or the common good, the fact that a debate would focus on these concepts helps to provide a framework for discussion, and may help to shape the ultimate decision.

The flexibility of the social doctrine may lead some to be uncomfortable or frustrated, since they look to the Church for clear and direct answers to the issues that concern them, especially moral questions. Obviously, for a great number of moral issues, the Church can offer such clarity — there is usually little room for ambiguity, for instance, in the practical application of the Fifth Commandment in an individual's daily life. In fact, there are a number of areas in which the social doctrine does provide clear answers, as it does with threats to the sanctity of human life such as legalized abortion and euthanasia. But in many cases, since the political realm involves the delicate balancing of many countervailing concerns, the direct application of the Church's social teaching to pragmatic issues is not clearcut.

The question arises, then, as to what principles would be relevant in applying Catholic social teaching to present-day concerns. To aid discussion of this point, I have selected four issues, along with some suggested principles of the social doctrine one may use in developing particular policy recommendations. I tried to choose issues that are not in the headlines today, in order to make it easier to look at them from a fresh perspective. For each issue, it would be useful to consider what could or should be done by the following potential actors: the pastor of a local parish, his parish council, the diocesan bishop, the state or national bishops' conference, individual Catholic lay persons (especially journalists and professionals in the affected field), Catholic public officials, and Catholic organizations.

The goal of this kind of discussion is to offer a new way of looking at various policy debates. We have become accustomed to seeing policy positions neatly labeled as either "liberal" or "conservative." However accurate such a classification may be, it tends to encourage a reflexive and even stereotyped response that is inevitably tinged with partisan motives. Indeed, public policy debates have become increasingly a battle of sound bites and propaganda, rather than a measured consideration of substance and principle. Addressing these issues from the standpoint of the Church's social doctrine, however, can illustrate how a distinctively Catholic voice can be added to the public debate on these issues, and how the Gospel may help to build a better society for all.

WELFARE REFORM

There have been many efforts on the state and national levels to change the system under which social welfare programs provide benefits to recipients. Common elements of these proposals include limits on the amount of time one can receive benefits, requirements that some recipients perform work as a condition of benefits (so-called "workfare"), a limit on the amount of benefits based on the size of a family ("family caps"), fingerprinting requirements to address allegations of fraud, and limits on the amount of benefits for out-of-state residents. Another typical proposal has been to reduce the role of the federal and state governments by devolving responsibility for designing and administering programs upon the states or localities.

79

Some of the principles of Catholic social teaching that may apply to this issue could include: concern for the common good; respect for human dignity; the special duty to care for the poor; the principles of subsidiarity, social justice and solidarity; the right and obligation to work; the centrality of the family in society; the freedom of parents to determine the size of their families; the duty of parents to support their children through productive activity; the responsibilities of public authorities to support families and to ensure living conditions that foster genuine human development; the role and importance of intermediary organizations (e.g., churches, and private social service agencies).

SCHOOL AND HOUSING DESEGREGATION

In the early 1980's, a lawsuit was brought against the city of Yonkers, New York, alleging that racial discrimination had produced illegal segregation of both schools and public housing. During the course of a very contentious process, a federal court found the city liable for discrimination, and implemented a remedy that involved re-districting of schools, busing of children, and the construction of low-income housing in primarily white neighborhoods. During the course of the litigation, the city was split into acrimonious camps, including a great deal of opposition to the busing of children from neighborhood schools. There was also much political turmoil as some city officials openly resisted the orders of the federal court (indeed, the resistance of the city government culminated in an unprecedented citation for contempt of court, which was upheld by the Supreme Court).

Some of the principles of Catholic social teaching that may

apply to this issue could include: the condemnation of racism; solidarity and the fundamental unity of the human family; the duty of the government to ensure housing for all citizens; the obligation of society and public authorities to redress past injustices, to foster unity in society, and to eradicate economic and social disparity between individuals and peoples; the right of parents to direct and oversee the education of their children; the duty of all citizens to obey the lawfully constituted authorities; the right to own and use private property, consistent with the obligations of solidarity and social justice; subsidiarity and the question of the appropriate level of government that should be responsible for the relevant public policy.

MOUNTAINTOP MINING

In recent years, many firms in the coal mining industry have begun to use a technique known as "mountaintop removal mining," which involves scraping away layers of rock from the top of mountains to reach coal seams hundreds of feet under the surface. The rock and dirt from the mine are dumped in nearby valleys, where they frequently bury streams. Current federal law permits this technique, provided that the firm reclaims the land that is mined by landscaping, replanting grass, trees, etc. Environmental groups have attempted to block the use of this mining method, but both mining companies and the unions support its use, claiming that it is an economically feasible way to create employment in the mining and related industries (e.g., trucking, maintenance, etc.).

Some of the principles of Catholic social teaching that may apply to this issue could include: the duty of environmental stewardship; the right and duty to provide an income for one's family; the role and importance of intermediary organizations (e.g., labor unions, issue advocacy associations); the need for sustainable and enduring economic development that addresses a full range of human needs rather than short-term interests; the responsibility of the government to regulate the economy for the common good and to ensure the opportunity for economic initiative.

IMMIGRATION AND REFUGEES

The regulation of immigration into the United States, and the proper treatment of those who seek refuge within our borders, has been an important issue for much of American history. In the past few years, there have been a number of politically charged debates over proposals to restrict immigration and to deny social service benefits to immigrants. One such proposal, a ballot initiative in California (Proposition 187), was specifically aimed at those who were in the United States in violation of the immigration laws (for whom the Church prefers the term "undocumented immigrants," rather than the pejorative phrase "illegal aliens"). The initiative, which was adopted after an extremely divisive campaign, denies public education to their children and prohibits them from access to publicly-financed social and health care services. Other recent proposals would restrict the preferences granted to persons who wish to move to the United States to join their families, reduce the number of refugees who will be admitted, and require employers to obtain proof of citizenship or lawful immigration status.

Some of the principles of Catholic social teaching that may apply to this issue could include: the principles of solidarity and the unity of the human family; the obligation to work for the common good of all mankind; the universal destination of goods for all mankind; the duty of more prosperous nations to welcome immigrants, subject to reasonable conditions; the right to religious and civil liberty, to due process of the laws, and to protection against oppression; the duty of society to support families, to ensure access to what is needed to lead a truly human life, and to foster genuine human development; the right to work in humane and fair conditions; the right and duty of civil authorities to ensure the stability and security within their borders.

ST PAULS

This book was designed and published by St. Pauls/Alba House, the publishing arm of the Society of St. Paul, an international religious congregation of priests and brothers dedicated to serving the Church through the communications media. For information regarding this and associated ministries of the Pauline Family of Congregations, write to the Vocation Director, Society of St. Paul, 7050 Pinehurst, Dearborn, Michigan 48126. Phone (313) 582-3798 or check our internet site, www.albahouse.org